Meredith Levy   Sarah Ackroyd

Messages

Teacher's Resource Pack

1

CAMBRIDGE
UNIVERSITY PRESS

CAMBRIDGE UNIVERSITY PRESS
Cambridge, New York, Melbourne, Madrid, Cape Town, Singapore, São Paulo

Cambridge University Press
The Edinburgh Building, Cambridge CB2 2RU, UK

www.cambridge.org
Information on this title: www.cambridge.org/9780521614269

First published 2005

Printed in the United Kingdom at the University Press, Cambridge.

A catalogue record for this publication is available from the British Library

ISBN-13 978-0-521-61426-9 Teacher's Resource Pack
ISBN-10 0-521-61426-0 Teacher's Resource Pack

ISBN-13 978-0-521-54707-9 Student's Book
ISBN-10 0-521-54707-5 Student's Book

ISBN-13 978-0-521-54708-6 Workbook with Audio CD
ISBN-10 0-521-54708-3 Workbook with Audio CD

ISBN-13 978-0-521-61425-2 Teacher's Book
ISBN-10 0-521-61425-2 Teacher's Book

ISBN-13 978-0-521-61427-6 Class Cassettes
ISBN-10 0-521-61427-9 Class Cassettes

ISBN-13 978-0-521-61428-3 Class Audio CDs
ISBN-10 0-521-61428-7 Class Audio CDs

Contents

Introduction

The Teacher's Resource Pack for *Messages* Level 1 contains a range of photocopiable materials for you to use with your classes. It will help provide a complete set of materials for the classroom, with further resources available on the *Messages* website, www.cambridge.org/elt/messages

The Teacher's Resource Pack contains the following elements:

- Introduction with tests marking scheme
- Entry test and answer key
- Pattern drills
- Teaching notes and answer keys for the photocopiable activities
- Photocopiable communication activities and grammar exercises
- Module tests
- Final test
- Test answer keys

The contents are organised by these main areas, with each of the sections marked by a grey side label for easy reference.

Entry test

The entry test is for use at the beginning of the course and has been designed with two purposes. It can be used purely as a diagnostic entry test – there are straightforward language exercises to check how much students have retained from their previous learning – or it can be used to provide extra remedial practice.

Pattern drills

The pattern drills are designed to give students clearly staged practice of formulating newly learnt structures orally, thereby helping them to gain confidence before attempting to use the structures in a freer context. There is a drill for every key area of language taught in the course (there are none for Unit 1 as it is a revision unit), and some Steps contain two drills. You may therefore wish to use them before the *Use what you know* activities in the corresponding steps. The Teacher's Book notes indicate where we would suggest using them in each case. Alternatively, you may wish to use them at a later stage as revision.

Recordings of the pattern drills are on the Workbook CD (tracks 14–37). The example sentence is recorded twice so that students can hear it with the response and then formulate it themselves. In all the pattern drills, there is a brief pause between the prompt and the response for you to pause the CD and allow students to say the sentence before they hear it. As students will have a copy of the CD in their Workbook, you can encourage them to repeat the pattern drills at home to reinforce the language they have learnt in class.

Teaching notes for the photocopiable activities

These contain clear step-by-step instructions for all the activities. In addition, there are answers for the communication activities where relevant and answers for all of the grammar practice exercises.

Photocopiable communication activities and grammar exercises

The communication activities reflect the key grammar and/or vocabulary in each unit. They are designed to activate new language in a communicative context. They cover a range of fun and motivating activity types, for example, board games, quizzes, information gap activities, descriptions, etc.

The grammar exercises cover specific areas of the key grammar from each unit. They are intended for fast finishers or students who need extra practice.

Mixed-ability classes: if you have a mixed-ability class and your students need further remedial practice, please log onto our website www.cambridge.org/elt/messages where you can download easier grammar exercises. There are four of these exercises for every unit in the book.

Module tests

Please see page 5 for a full marking scheme.

This section contains six module tests. Each of the tests covers one module (two units) in the Student's Book.

Each test consists of six parts:

Grammar (20 marks): this is divided into two sections (a and b), with ten marks each. Activity types vary, but include:

- Completing discrete, gapped sentences by selecting one word from three choices provided or by choosing from words in a box. Both of these activities are designed to test understanding of key language at sentence level.
- Writing the correct verb forms from a list of infinitives, or complete sentences using the correct tense, for example. This part is designed to test students' knowledge and use of key verb forms they have studied.
- Changing the form of the verb from affirmative to negative, in order to test their ability to apply the grammar of a language point across its various forms.

Vocabulary (20 marks): is also divided into two sections (a and b) with ten marks each. Activity types vary, but include:

- Completing discrete, gapped sentences by selecting one word from three choices provided or by choosing from words in a box. These test students' ability to use new vocabulary in the correct contexts.

- Spelling a word by placing the letters in the correct order, or completing the missing letters of a word after reading a clue. Both of these activities test students' ability to spell and to recognise words on an individual level.
- Labelling illustrations. This tests students' ability to identify lexis, as well as spelling the word correctly.
- Choosing which word does not belong in a closed group of four. This tests students' ability to focus on the connections between words and encourages them to think of vocabulary in terms of related areas.

Reading (10 marks): in each of these sections there is one text with one set of comprehension questions. These may be true/false statements, writing questions for given answers, or open questions, for example. They are designed to test students on the type of sub-skills practised in the Student's Book, for example, reading for specific information, or gist.

Writing (10 marks): in this section students write a reply to a prompt such as an email or letter from an imaginary penfriend and must include specific topics in their answers.

Listening (10 marks): the listening section is divided into two sections. Students listen to one extract, a dialogue, a monologue or several speakers, which is played at least twice. There are two sets of questions. In questions 1–5, students are tested on their general understanding, for example, the topics discussed or the speakers' attitudes. In this section, students may have to tick the topics discussed from a given list, or write down the names of key vocabulary mentioned, for example. Questions 6–10 require more detailed comprehension and test students' ability to listen for specific information. They may be required to answer specific questions or choose from true/false statements.

NB The recordings for the listening tests are on the Class Cassettes/CDs, at the end of each module.

Speaking (10 marks): this section is divided into two sections (a and b). In part a, students are required to answer specific questions asked by you. These always start with greetings, and are followed by questions based on topics and language covered in the modules. They are designed to help students activate the language they have learnt and demonstrate their knowledge of the key vocabulary and grammar. In part b students work with another student to complete a designated task based on prompt cards. The speaking section of the test includes both the instructions for the teachers and the prompt cards for the students. In most cases you will only need to copy one page for every two students.

Final test

The final test has the same format and marks available as the modular tests, but tests language from all parts of the course. As its name suggests, it is designed to be done upon completion of the course, and may therefore be used as an end-of-year test.

Examinations

The modular tests and final test of *Messages* have been designed to provide useful preparation for students taking public examinations such as UCLES KET and Trinity Integrated Skills.

Test keys

These are positioned at the end of each test and include tapescripts for the listening tests.

Test marking scheme

The answer key to the entry test is on page 10. The marking scheme is straightforward and the number of marks awarded is written at the end of each exercise.

Each of the modular tests and the final test have six components and there are 80 marks available. Each test follows the same format:

Section 1	Grammar	20 marks
Section 2	Vocabulary	20 marks
Section 3	Reading	10 marks
Section 4	Writing	10 marks
Section 5	Listening	10 marks
Section 6	Speaking	10 marks

How to mark Section 4 Writing

Each item has a maximum of five marks, giving a total of ten marks. Marks should be awarded according to two main criteria:

- Relevant content. Has the student answered the question fully and included all the given topics? (5 marks)
- Appropriate use of grammar and vocabulary, including spelling. (5 marks)

How to mark Section 6 Speaking

In each of the two sections, give each student a mark based on overall performance. Marks should be awarded according to two main criteria:

- Task completion: have they included the main points in their prompts? Have their responses been relevant? Have they managed to communicate their ideas successfully, without too many misunderstandings? (5 marks)
- Appropriate use of grammar and vocabulary. (5 marks)

In section b, where the two students talk to each other, it is important to judge each separately: for example, if Student B is weak, this should not affect the mark of a stronger Student A.

The marks should be recorded on the Listening page of each student's test in the box labelled 'Speaking'.

Name ....

Class .... Date ....

1 Grammar

a Complete the sentences with the words in the box.

'm   ~~live~~   've got   can   's got   's   's   're   like   don't   do

0   I _____ live _____ in Barcelona.

1   My name _____ Jodie.

2   I _____ two brothers.

3   _____ you help me?

4   I _____ understand.

5   How _____ you spell 'teacher'?

6   My sister _____ brown hair.

7   Do you _____ football?

8   Jack _____ my friend.

9   I _____ from Italy.

10 We _____ on holiday in France.

|10|

b Put the words in the right order and make questions.

0   your / I / can / dictionary / use ?

  Can I use your dictionary? _____

1   today / what / date / the / 's ?

  _____

2   you / are / how ?

  _____

3   's / name / what / your ?

  _____

4   live / where / you / do ?

  _____

5   from / where / you / are ?

  _____

6   'table' / what / mean / does ?

  _____

7   are / old / you / how ?

  _____

8   'cat' / you / can / spell ?

  _____

9   birthday / 's / your / when ?

  _____

10 got / bike / a / you / have ?

  _____

|10|

c Complete the sentences with *am, is* or *are*.

0 My teacher ....*is*......... American.

1 We .... at school.

2 Where .... my dictionary?

3 What .... it?

4 I .... eleven years old.

5 .... you OK?

6 We .... students.

7 Murray .... my brother.

8 Susan and Sarah .... my friends.

9 I .... from Spain.

10 John .... English.

[10]

d Match the questions with the answers.

0 How do you spell your name?	a	No, I'm not. I'm American.
1 How are you?	b	Fine, thanks.
2 Can you help me?	c	Yes, he is.
3 What's your address?	d	1st January.
4 Where are you from?	e	Yes, thanks.
5 What's the time?	f	Sure.
6 When's your birthday?	g	P-A-O-L-A
7 Are you English?	h	France.
8 Are you OK?	i	No, I don't.
9 Do you understand?	j	17 Wisbeach Rd, Southwold.
10 Is John your brother?	k	It's eleven o'clock.

0 ..*g*.. 1 ...... 2 ...... 3 ...... 4 ...... 5 ...... 6 ...... 7 ...... 8 ...... 9 ...... 10 ......

[10]

Grammar	40

2 Vocabulary

a Things in the classroom. Label the objects.

0 _____window_____

1 _____

2 _____

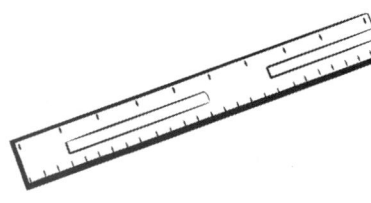

3 _____

4 _____

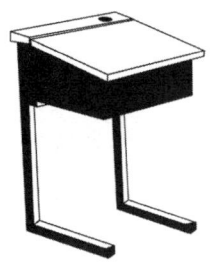

5 _____

6 _____

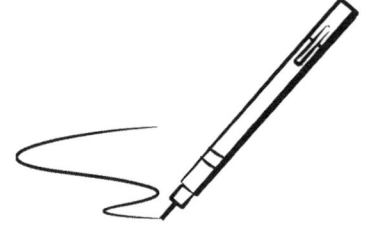

7 _____

8 _____

9 _____

10 _____

| 10 |

b Numbers. Write the words.

0 3 _____three_____

1 5 _____
2 12 _____
3 20 _____
4 11 _____
5 8 _____

6 15 _____
7 22 _____
8 13 _____
9 2 _____
10 6 _____

| 10 |

Name ....

Class .... Date ....

c Write the months of the year.

1 _January_   5 ....   9 ....

2 _February_   6 ....   10 ....

3 ....   7 ....   11 ....

4 ....   8 ....   12 ....

[10]

d Food. Label the pictures.

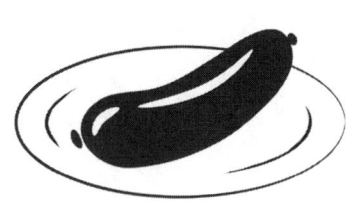  

0 _sausage_   1 ....   2 ....

3 ....   4 ....   5 ....

6 ....   7 ....   8 ....

9 ....   10 ....

	[10]
Vocabulary	40
Test total	80

1 Grammar

a 1 's   2 've got   3 Can   4 don't   5 do   6 's got   7 like   8 's   9 'm   10 're

b 1 What's the date today?
2 How are you?
3 What's your name?
4 Where do you live?
5 Where are you from?
6 What does 'table' mean?
7 How old are you?
8 Can you spell 'cat'?
9 When's your birthday?
10 Have you got a bike?

c 1 are/'re   2 is/'s   3 is   4 am/'m   5 Are   6 are/'re   7 is/'s   8 are   9 am/'m   10 is/'s

d 1 b   2 f   3 j   4 h   5 k   6 d   7 a   8 e   9 i   10 c

2 Vocabulary

a 1 book   2 dictionary   3 ruler   4 pencil   5 desk   6 computer   7 pen   8 bag   9 poster
10 teacher

b 1 five   2 twelve   3 twenty   4 eleven   5 eight   6 fifteen   7 twenty-two   8 thirteen   9 two
10 six

c 3 March   4 April   5 May   6 June   7 July   8 August   9 September   10 October   11 November
12 December

d 1 banana   2 sandwich   3 ice cream   4 apple   5 orange   6 bread   7 fish   8 pizza
9 chips / french fries   10 salad

Unit 2 Step 2

be: questions and short answers

🔊 Listen to the questions and give true answers. For example:

Are you English?
No, I'm not.

Are you in England?
Are you at school?
Is it Monday today?
Is it Tuesday?
Is it Wednesday?
Is Sydney the capital of Australia?
Is Milan the capital of Italy?
Are you sure?

Unit 3 Step 1

1 *have got:* negative

🔊 You haven't got any of these things. Listen to the example, then answer the questions.

Can I borrow your calculator?
Sorry, I haven't got a calculator.

Can I borrow your tennis racket?
Sorry, I haven't got a tennis racket.

I need a baseball cap. Can you help?
Sorry, I haven't got a baseball cap.

I need some football socks. Can you help?
Sorry, I haven't got any football socks.

I'm hungry. Can I share your crisps?
Sorry, I haven't got any crisps.

Can I borrow your rubber?
Sorry, I haven't got a rubber.

2 *have got:* questions and short answers

🔊 Imagine you're talking to a new friend. Listen to the example, then ask questions with *Have you got?*.

dog
Have you got a dog?

pets
Have you got any pets?

brothers or sisters
Have you got any brothers or sisters?

a CD player
Have you got a CD player?

a computer
Have you got a computer?

computer games
Have you got any computer games?

Unit 3 Step 2

Possessive ´s

🔊 Listen to the questions and talk about Sadie. For example:

Who's Joe?
He's Sadie's brother.

Who's Kate?
She's Sadie's sister.

Who's Mr Kelly?
He's Sadie's father.

Who's Mrs Kelly?
She's Sadie's mother.

Who's Annie?
She's Sadie's cousin.

Who's Jack?
He's Sadie's friend.

Unit 4 Step 1

What's he/she/it like? What are they like?

🔊 Listen to the example, then answer the questions.

What's that game like? (difficult)
It's really difficult.

What's Sadie's brother like? (nice)
He's really nice.

What's Lisa like? (great)
She's really great.

What's that book like? (good)
It's really good.

What are Lee and Barney like? (funny)
They're really funny.

What's that video like? (boring)
It's really boring.

Please note that the audio material for these Pattern drills is on the Workbook CD.

Unit 4 Step 2

He´s/She´s got

🔊 The Kellys are at the shops. Listen to the example, then answer the questions.

What's Joe got? (a new CD)
He´s got a new CD.

What's Sadie got? (a new computer game)
She´s got a new computer game.

What's Mr Kelly got? (some new trainers)
He´s got some new trainers.

What's Mrs Kelly got? (a new tennis racket)
She´s got a new tennis racket.

What's Kate got? (a new camera)
She´s got a new camera.

Unit 5 Step 1

Present simple: third person *s*

🔊 Sadie and her friend Lisa are similar in a lot of ways. Listen to Sadie, then make sentences about Lisa. For example:

I like horror films.
Lisa likes horror films too.

I play tennis.
Lisa plays tennis too.

I love pizza.
Lisa loves pizza too.

I talk a lot.
Lisa talks a lot too.

I believe in ghosts.
Lisa believes in ghosts too.

I go to the judo club.
Lisa goes to the judo club too.

Unit 5 Step 2

1 Present simple: questions

🔊 Listen to the example, then ask more questions.

ghosts
Do you believe in ghosts?

aliens
Do you believe in aliens?

UFOs
Do you believe in UFOs?

vampires
Do you believe in vampires?

Father Christmas
Do you believe in Father Christmas?

2 Present simple: questions and short answers

🔊 Listen to the example, then answer the questions.

Do Joe and Sadie live in Exeter?
Yes, they do.

Does Jack live in Exeter?
Yes, he does.

Does he play in Joe's band?
No, he doesn't.

Does he go to school with Sadie?
Yes, he does.

Do they walk to school?
No, they don't.

Do they go on the bus?
Yes, they do.

Unit 6 Step 2

Food vocabulary; present simple: negative

🔊 Listen to the example, then answer with *Sorry, I don't like ... .*

Have some cheese!
Sorry, I don't like cheese.

Have some orange juice!
Sorry, I don't like orange juice.

Have some sausages!
Sorry, I don't like sausages.

Have some chicken!
Sorry, I don't like chicken.

Have some fish!
Sorry, I don't like fish.

Have some pasta!
Sorry, I don't like pasta.

Have some vegetables!
Sorry, I don't like vegetables.

Unit 6 Step 3

Daily routines; frequency adverbs

🔊 Listen to the example, then say the sentences, using the frequency adverbs.

I get up at seven. (usually)
I usually get up at seven.

I have a shower. (always)
I always have a shower.

I have breakfast at seven thirty. (usually)
I usually have breakfast at seven thirty.

Please note that the audio material for these Pattern drills is on the Workbook CD.

PATTERN DRILLS

I have some toast. (always)
I always have some toast.

I have some fruit juice. (*sometimes)
I sometimes have some fruit juice.

I go to school by bus. (usually)
I usually go to school by bus.

The bus is late. (*sometimes)
The bus is sometimes late.

(*Note: the position of *sometimes* can vary.
It is also possible to say *Sometimes I have ...*
and *I have some fruit juice sometimes.*)

Unit 7 Step 2

① ### *There is/are:* questions and short answers

🔊 Listen to the questions about your school and give true answers. For example:

Is there a gym at your school?
Yes, there is.

Is there a swimming pool?
Are there any showers?
Is there a shop?
Are there any English people?
Is there a dining room?
Are there any tennis courts?
Is there a garden?

② ### *There is/are* + countable and uncountable nouns

🔊 Listen to the example, then make sentences with *There's some* or *There are some.* All the things are in the cupboard.

I want some coffee.
There's some coffee in the cupboard.

Have we got any tea?
There's some tea in the cupboard.

I can't find the onions.
There are some onions in the cupboard.

Have we got any pasta?
There's some pasta in the cupboard.

What about tomatoes?
There are some tomatoes in the cupboard.

And I need some eggs.
There are some eggs in the cupboard.

Unit 8 Step 1

can for abilities

🔊 Listen and talk about the things that Buzz can do. For example:

ski
He can ski.

sing
He can sing.

ride a horse
He can ride a horse.

swim
He can swim.

play the keyboard
He can play the keyboard.

speak Spanish
He can speak Spanish.

Unit 8 Step 2

Can you see/hear ...? + short answers

🔊 Listen to the questions about your classroom and give true answers. For example:

When you're in your classroom, can you see any trees?
Yes, we can.

Can you see any shops?
Can you hear the traffic?
Can you hear any trains?
Can you see any flats?
Can you hear any birds?

Unit 8 Step 3

must/mustn't

🔊 Listen to these commands. Repeat them using *You must* or *You mustn't.* For example:

Go to bed!
You must go to bed.

Don't be rude!
You mustn't be rude.

Don't be silly!
You mustn't be silly.

Be quiet!
You must be quiet.

Don't do that!
You mustn't do that.

Don't panic!
You mustn't panic.

Say it in English!
You must say it in English.

Unit 9 Step 1

Present continuous: affirmative

🔊 **Listen and say what everyone is doing. For example:**

Joe and Barney are in front of the television. (watch)
They're watching television.

Joe's got some crisps. (eat)
He's eating some crisps.

Barney's got some lemonade. (drink)
He's drinking some lemonade.

Mrs Kelly's got a magazine in her hand. (read)
She's reading a magazine.

Lisa and Sadie are at the shops. (do their shopping)
They're doing their shopping.

Mel's in the shower. (have)
She's having a shower.

Lee's on his bike. (ride)
He's riding his bike.

Unit 9 Step 2

1 Present continuous: negative

🔊 **These sentences aren't true. Listen and put them into the negative. For example:**

Jack's going to bed.
He isn't going to bed.

Mel's having her lunch.
She isn't having her lunch.

Joe and Barney are going to school.
They aren't going to school.

Mrs Kelly's going to work.
She isn't going to work.

Sadie and Lisa are shouting.
They aren't shouting.

Lee's listening to the radio.
He isn't listening to the radio.

2 Object pronouns

🔊 **Sadie's looking for things, but she can't find them. What does she say? Listen to the example, then continue.**

I'm looking for my green T-shirt.
I can't find it.

I'm looking for my glasses.
I can't find them.

I'm looking for Dad.
I can't find him.

I'm looking for my trainers.
I can't find them.

I'm looking for Lisa.
I can't find her.

I'm looking for my watch.
I can't find it.

I'm looking for Joe and Jack.
I can't find them.

Unit 10 Step 1

Present continuous for future arrangements

🔊 **Listen and describe Sadie's arrangements for tomorrow. For example:**

she / go to the beach
She's going to the beach.

she / go with Lisa
She's going with Lisa.

they / catch the bus
They're catching the bus.

they / leave at nine
They're leaving at nine.

they / take their lunch
They're taking their lunch.

they / go swimming
They're going swimming.

they / meet some friends
They're meeting some friends.

Unit 10 Step 2

going to

🔊 **What are they going to buy? Listen to the example, then make more sentences with *going to*.**

Jack / a plastic dinosaur
Jack's going to buy a plastic dinosaur.

Ben / a plastic whale
Ben's going to buy a plastic whale.

I / a T-shirt
I'm going to buy a T-shirt.

we / some postcards
We're going to buy some postcards.

Lisa and Sadie / some posters
Lisa and Sadie are going to buy some posters.

Mr White / a pen
Mr White's going to buy a pen.

Please note that the audio material for these Pattern drills is on the Workbook CD.

Unit 11 Step 1

was/were

🔊 Where were the Kellys at seven o'clock last night? Listen and make sentences with *was* and *were*. For example:

Kate / on her houseboat
Kate was on her houseboat.

Joe and Sadie / at home
Joe and Sadie were at home.

Sadie / in the bath
Sadie was in the bath.

Joe / in his room
Joe was in his room.

Mr Kelly / in the kitchen
Mr Kelly was in the kitchen.

Mrs Kelly / at a friend's house
Mrs Kelly was at a friend's house.

Unit 11 Step 3

Past simple: regular verbs

🔊 Listen and talk about things that happened yesterday. For example:

Do you play football every day?
Well, I played football yesterday.

Do you watch TV every day?
Well, I watched TV yesterday.

Do you walk to school every day?
Well, I walked to school yesterday.

Do you arrive late every day?
Well, I arrived late yesterday.

Do you cook the dinner every day?
Well, I cooked the dinner yesterday.

Do you clean your teeth every day?
Well, I cleaned my teeth yesterday.

Unit 12 Step 2

Past simple: irregular verbs

🔊 Listen to the sentences about what Joe did yesterday, then ask questions about Ben. For example:

Joe went to London.
Did Ben go to London?

Joe saw the match.
Did Ben see the match?

Joe left in the morning.
Did Ben leave in the morning?

Joe went on the train.
Did Ben go on the train?

Joe had a burger.
Did Ben have a burger?

Joe came back last night.
Did Ben come back last night?

Unit 1

Grammar practice key

1
2 My name's Lisa.
3 Can you help me, please?
4 I'm twelve and I've got two brothers.
5 How do you spell it?
6 Do you understand?
7 Can you say that again, please?
8 I live in Paris.

2 2 g 3 e 4 c 5 h 6 f 7 b 8 a

3 2 Her 3 He 4 His 5 He 6 She 7 Her 8 His

4
2 All right, thanks.
3 I'm thirteen.
4 It's a tortoise.
5 Sadie Kelly.
6 I'm Argentinian.
7 In London.
8 It's 15th August.

Communication activity

- To practise the language in this unit and to reinforce information about the characters, use the board game on pages 22–23. The game can be played by two, three or four players. Each group will need a copy of the board on page 22 and the set of questions on page 23, cut up into separate cards. Players will also need counters or coins to move around the board.

- The question cards are placed face down in a pile. Players each place their counter on a different Home square. The aim is to be the first person to move round the board and arrive back at their Home square.

- Student A picks up a card and asks Student B the question. If B makes a correct and appropriate answer, he/she moves along the number of squares written on the card. It is then B's turn to ask a question, and so the game continues. Any of the players can challenge an answer if they think it is incorrect but, if their challenge is wrong, they move back one space.

- Monitor the groups and help with any vocabulary problems on the question cards. The number of cards should be sufficient to last through the game. If they run out, students can shuffle them and start again.

Unit 2

Grammar practice key

1
2 He's / He is 3 They're / They are
4 You're / You are 5 I'm / I am 6 It's / It is
7 We're / We are 8 she's / she is

2 2 d 3 h 4 a 5 g 6 c 7 e 8 b

3
2 they aren't / they're not 3 she isn't / she's not 4 I'm not 5 they aren't / they're not 6 he isn't / he's not 7 it isn't / it's not 8 we aren't / we're not

4
2 Is; she is 3 Is; he isn't / he's not 4 Are; I am 5 Are; they aren't / they're not 6 Is; it is 7 Is; she isn't / she's not 8 Are; I'm not

Communication activity

- For further practice of *be* and to revise the vocabulary of Unit 2, hold a class quiz using the questions on page 25. Photocopy the questions, cut them up and put them in a bag. Divide the class into teams of four or five and ask them to appoint one person to write the team answers on a piece of paper.

- Students take it in turns to pick a question from the bag and read it aloud to the class and give the question number. Teams confer briefly (and quietly) to agree on the answer, using the short answer form (*Yes, it is, No, they aren't*, etc.). For *No* answers, they should add a correct statement if they can.

- After a round of six questions, teams hand their answer sheets to another group to mark. The teacher checks the answers with the class. The scoring system is:

  - 1 point for the correct answer *Yes* or *No*
  - 1 point for the correct short answer form
  - 1 point for a correction to a *No* answer

  They then receive their sheets back and continue with the next round of questions. The top scorers at the end of the four rounds are the winners.

Unit 3

Grammar practice key

1 2 some 3 an 4 a 5 some 6 an 7 some
8 a, a

2
2 They've got some books.
3 Have you got any crisps?
4 We haven't got any cousins.
5 Have they got any photos?
6 I haven't got any tissues.
7 We've got some badges.
8 They haven't got any friends.

3 2 Diana's 3 Lee's 4 your friend's
5 his father's 6 your cat's 7 Bill and Clare's 8 your aunt and uncle's

4 2 my 3 His 4 Our 5 Her 6 their
7 your 8 his

Communication activity

- For further practice of possessive 's and *have got* + *a*/*an*/*some*, and to revise the vocabulary of Unit 3, use the activity on page 27. Make photocopies of the page and cut them into A and B sheets for each pair in the class.

- Students take it in turns to give information about the completed pictures on their sheet, focusing on what the person has got in his/her bag, hand and lunchbox. Their partner draws in the missing details in their picture. Pairs compare their sentences and discuss any differences between them.

- They can work together on the sentences, using their pictures to choose the correct words.

Answers

1 Greg   2 Sarah   3 Greg   4 are   5 There isn't
6 Greg's   7 hasn't

Unit 4
Grammar practice key

1 2 short hair   3 tall man   4 (very) friendly dog
5 brown eyes   6 new surfboard
7 dangerous animals   8 long, curly hair

2 2 hasn't got   3 's got   4 hasn't got
5 hasn't got   6 's got   7 's got   8 hasn't got

3 2 Has she got a cold?
she has
3 Has Richard got a bike?
he hasn't
4 Have you and Helen got any videos?
we have
5 Have your parents got a big car?
they haven't
6 Have horses got long legs?
they have

4 2 Linda – Linda's   3 has – have
4 Are – Have   5 not has – hasn't
6 Is – Has   7 isn't – haven't   8 Has – Have

Communication activity

- For further practice in describing people, use the information gap activity on page 29. Make photocopies of the page and cut them into A and B sheets for each pair in the class.

- Students take it in turns to describe the people in the completed picture on their sheet. Their partner draws in the details missing from their incomplete picture. Encourage them to ask questions for clarification if they need to. At the end, pairs compare their pictures and discuss any differences between them.

Unit 5
Grammar practice key

1 2 read   3 live   4 goes   5 write   6 plays
7 wears   8 use

2 2 loves   3 watch   4 doesn't eat
5 don't play   6 goes   7 want   8 doesn't come

3 2 Do, believe; I don't   3 Does, watch; she does
4 Do, read; they don't   5 Does, play; he does
6 Does, come; he doesn't   7 Do, wear; we don't
8 Do, eat; they do

4 2 What   3 Where   4 When   5 Why

Communication activity

- For further practice of the present simple, use the information gap activity on page 31. Make photocopies of the page and cut them into A and B sheets for each pair in the class.

- Students take it in turns to ask about the people and fill in the table. Both students then work together to complete the sentences, using information from the table.

Answers

1 Anna   2 Andrew   3 Laura   4 Anna
5 Anna, Andrew   6 Laura   7 Anna

Unit 6
Grammar practice key

1 2 I often tidy my room.
3 My parents always drink tea.
4 Pasta is usually popular.
5 Joe sometimes catches the bus to school.
6 Your dogs are always energetic.
7 Christine is usually hungry at lunchtime.
8 James never watches TV in the evening.

2 2 often is – is often   3 go usually – usually go
4 dos – does   5 don't – doesn't   6 drink always – always drink   7 haves – has
8 often are – are often

3 2 Patrick doesn't always watch TV after school.
3 She isn't usually on time.
4 Giraffes don't usually attack people.
5 We don't usually have eggs for breakfast.
6 Michael and Greg aren't often late for school.

4 2 Does Robert get up before Lisa?
Yes, he does.
3 Where does Robert have a shower?
At the swimming pool.
4 Does Lisa have a shower after breakfast?
No, she doesn't.

5   Do they walk to school?
    No, they don't.

6   What time do they get to school?
    At 8.40.

Communication activity

- For further practice of the present simple and to revise words for animals, use the crossword on page 33. Make photocopies of the page and cut them into A and B sheets for each pair in the class.

- Students take it in turns to ask about the missing animal words in their crossword. Their partner has to describe the animal without saying its name. Both students then work together to complete the sentences with the names of animals from the crossword and appropriate verbs.

Answers

2 Gorillas, live   3 shark, is   4 Lions, attack
5 Bears, sleep   6 horse, eats   7 Giraffes, live
8 dolphin, isn't

Unit 7
Grammar practice key

1 2 There's   3 There aren't   4 There isn't
    5 There are   6 There isn't   7 There aren't
    8 There's

2 2   Is there any cheese in the kitchen?
        there is

    3   Are there any books in your bag?
        there aren't

    4   Is there any fruit juice in the bottle?
        there isn't

    5   Are there any computers at your school?
        there are

    6   Is there any paper on your desk?
        there isn't

    7   Are there any shelves in the wardrobe?
        there aren't

    8   Is there any bread on the table?
        there is

3 2 some   3 a   4 any   5 a   6 any   7 some
    8 any

4 2 g   3 c   4 h   5 a   6 d   7 b   8 f

Communication activity

- For further practice of There is/are + a, some and any, use the 'spot the difference' activity on page 35. Make photocopies of the page and cut them into A and B sheets for each pair in the class.

- Remind students that they must not look at each other's pictures until they have completed the activity.

Answers
A
There are three chairs.
There's a clock on the cupboard.
There's a rug.
There isn't any butter on the table.
There are some onions. There aren't any apples.
There aren't any eggs.
There's some water. There isn't any fruit juice.

B
There are two chairs.
There's a clock on the small table.
There isn't a rug.
There's some butter on the table.
There aren't any onions. There are some apples.
There are some eggs.
There isn't any water. There's some fruit juice.

Unit 8
Grammar practice key

1 2 g   3 e   4 a   5 c   6 h   7 f   8 d

2 2 can't see   3 can buy   4 can catch
    5 can't go   6 can't go   7 can watch
    8 can get

3 2   You mustn't eat in class.
    3   You mustn't argue.
    4   You must answer the question.
    5   You must help me.
    6   You mustn't ride your bike here.
    7   You must practise the piano every day.
    8   You mustn't be rude.

4 2 get   3 Be   4 Don't go   5 Don't get   6 Go
    7 Don't be   8 Listen

Communication activity

- For further practice of can and to revise words for places in a town, use the information gap activity on page 37. Make photocopies of the page and cut them into A and B maps for each pair in the class.

- Students take it in turns to ask about the missing places on their map. Their partner has to describe the place without saying the name.

- When students have completed the activity they can check their answers by looking at each other's maps.

Unit 9
Grammar practice key

1 2 's having   3 'm wearing   4 're helping
    5 's looking   6 are sitting   7 's working
    8 are playing

2 2 isn't / 's not watching   3 aren't / 're not wearing   4 aren't / 're not playing   5 aren't / 're not listening   6 'm not reading   7 aren't / 're not doing   8 isn't / 's not riding

3 2 Is he writing an email?
No, he isn't.
3 Is she talking to her boyfriend?
Yes, she is.
4 What are you doing?
I'm cleaning my shoes.
5 Where's she studying?
In New York.
6 What's Jack doing?
He's playing the piano.
7 Are they sitting on the beach?
No, they aren't.
8 Why's Sadie smiling?
Because she's feeling happy.

4 2 him   3 it   4 me   5 them   6 us   7 her   8 them

Communication activity

- For further practice of the present continuous, use the information gap activity on page 39. Make photocopies of the page and cut them into A and B pictures for each pair in the class.
- Students take it in turns to ask about the people on their list and write the missing names in the picture. Their partner has to identify the people by describing what they are doing/wearing. They check answers by showing their pictures at the end.
- Both students then work together to read the sentences and work out the names of the other three people in the picture.

Unit 10

Grammar practice key

1 2 're meeting   3 's coming   4 'm catching   5 isn't / 's not studying   6 Are, going   7 'm not wearing   8 Is, having

2 2 f   3 g   4 h   5 a   6 e   7 d   8 b

3 2 're going to take   3 's going to have   4 're going to ask   5 isn't / 's not going to visit   6 'm not going to play   7 's going to meet   8 aren't going to watch

4 2 Is Sharon going to buy a new tennis racket?
she is
3 Are Maria and Carlo going to have lunch with us?

they aren't / they're not
4 Is Andrew going to walk to school?
he isn't / he's not
5 Are your friends going to come to the party?
they are
6 Are you going to fly to Rome?
I'm not / we aren't / we're not

Communication activity

- For further practice in talking about future arrangements, use the information gap activity on page 41. Make photocopies of the page and cut them into A and B sheets for each pair in the class.
- Students take it in turns to ask present continuous questions using the question words on their sheet. They write the missing information in Mel's diary.
- At the end of the activity, students compare their diaries and check that they have the same information.

Unit 11

Grammar practice key

1 2 were   3 wasn't   4 weren't   5 was   6 was   7 were   8 wasn't

2 2 were – was   3 Was – Were   4 where – were   5 he's – was he   6 born – was born   7 were – was   8 wasnt – wasn't

3 2 played   3 watched   4 studied   5 listened   6 tidied   7 carried   8 travelled

4 2 Where did you travel?
To Canada and the USA.
3 Who did she visit?
Her aunt and uncle.
4 What did they watch on TV?
A sports programme.
5 Where did she work?
In a supermarket.
6 What did they study at university?
Maths and science.
7 When did the concert finish?
At half past ten.
8 What did those people want?
To find the station.

Communication activity

- For further practice of the past simple (affirmative and negative), use the sentence-building activity on page 43 with pairs or groups of three. Photocopy the page for each pair/group, cut up the sentence parts and put them in an envelope.

- Students open their envelope and work together to make 18 sentences. There are nine sentence openings, but two possible endings (with *and* or *but*) for each. Students must find the appropriate endings for each sentence and fill in the missing word *and* or *but*. Sentence 1 has been done for them as an example.

Answers

2 Yesterday morning it was cloudy and in the afternoon it started to rain / but it wasn't cold.

3 There was a computer in Elizabeth's room and she used it to surf the Internet / but it didn't belong to her.

4 Paula worked at a hotel last summer and she saved a lot of money / but she didn't like the job.

5 Mike played football on Saturday and his parents watched the match / but he didn't score a goal.

6 There were some CDs in the shop and Sam decided to buy one for his sister / but they weren't very good.

7 Peter phoned Maria this morning and they talked for twenty minutes / but she didn't want to speak to him.

8 We were thirsty and we asked for some fruit juice / but there wasn't anything to drink.

9 Caroline stayed in England last year and she studied in London / but she didn't visit Scotland.

Unit 12

Grammar practice key

1
2 Did you wait outside the theatre?
I/we didn't

3 Did it rain last night?
it didn't

4 Did Karen study for the test?
she did

5 Did the children help with the housework?
they didn't

6 Did you and Ben go swimming yesterday?
we did

2 2 didn't want   3 talked   4 didn't stop
5 worked   6 didn't answer

3 2 left   3 went   4 bought   5 had   6 ate
7 spoke   8 knew

4 2 <u>not</u> – didn't   3 <u>not went</u> – didn't go
4 <u>spoke</u> – speak   5 <u>not had</u> – didn't have
6 <u>you bought</u> – did you buy   7 <u>didn't was</u> –

wasn't   8 <u>Jane came</u> – did Jane come

Communication activity

- For revision of Units 1–12, use the board game on pages 45–46. The game can be played by two or three players, with one other student acting as quizmaster. The players need a copy of the board on page 45, a dice, and counters or coins to move around the board. The quizmaster needs a copy of the questions on page 46.

- Players each place their counter on a different square numbered 1 (A, B or C). They have to move down their track to square 16 and then back up again. The aim is to be the first person to reach the Home square.

- Student A throws the dice and moves to the corresponding square. The quizmaster asks the question for Student A for that square. If A makes a good answer, he/she stays on the square. If the answer is incorrect, A has to move back one square. It is then B's turn to throw the dice, the quizmaster uses a question from the Student B set of questions, and so the game continues. If someone lands on the same square for a second time, he/she moves one square ahead. Anyone can challenge an answer if they think it is incorrect, with the quizmaster making the final decision if there is any disagreement. (They may need to refer to the Student's Book to check some answers.)

1 Punctuation

Write the sentences. Use the right punctuation.

1 what nationality are you

What nationality are you?

2 my name's lisa

3 can you help me please

4 i'm twelve and i've got two brothers

5 how do you spell it

6 do you understand

7 can you say that again please

8 i live in paris

2 Making sentences

Match the words in A with the words in B and make sentences.

A		B	
1	My name's	a	two cats.
2	I'm	b	music.
3	I	c	sister called Amy.
4	I've got a	d	Peter.
5	My address is	e	live in England.
6	My sister	f	is seventeen.
7	I like	g	thirteen.
8	I've got	h	12 Green Street, Cambridge.

1 __d__ 2 ____ 3 ____ 4 ____ 5 ____ 6 ____ 7 ____ 8 ____

3 *He, She, His, Her*

Complete the sentences with *He, She, His* or *Her*.

1 Paul is my brother. _____He_____'s eleven.

2 She's my sister. _____ name's Sue.

3 Danny is a boy in my class. _____'s fourteen.

4 This is my friend. _____ name's David.

5 Jack lives in Exeter. _____'s English.

6 This is Kate. _____'s at university.

7 My friend Anna is twelve. _____ address is 32 New Road, Exeter.

8 This is Tom. _____ brother is in my class.

4 Questions and answers

Write answers to the questions. Use the answers in the box.

> I'm thirteen. Sadie Kelly. ~~Sure.~~
> I'm Argentinian. All right, thanks.
> It's 15th August. It's a tortoise.
> In London.

1 A: Can I use your pencil, please?

   B: *Sure.*

2 A: How are you?

   B: _____

3 A: How old are you?

   B: _____

4 A: Look at this animal! What is it?

   B: _____

5 A: What's her name?

   B: _____

6 A: What nationality are you?

   B: _____

7 A: Where do you live?

   B: _____

8 A: What's the date today?

   B: _____

RESOURCES UNIT 1

GRAMMAR PRACTICE

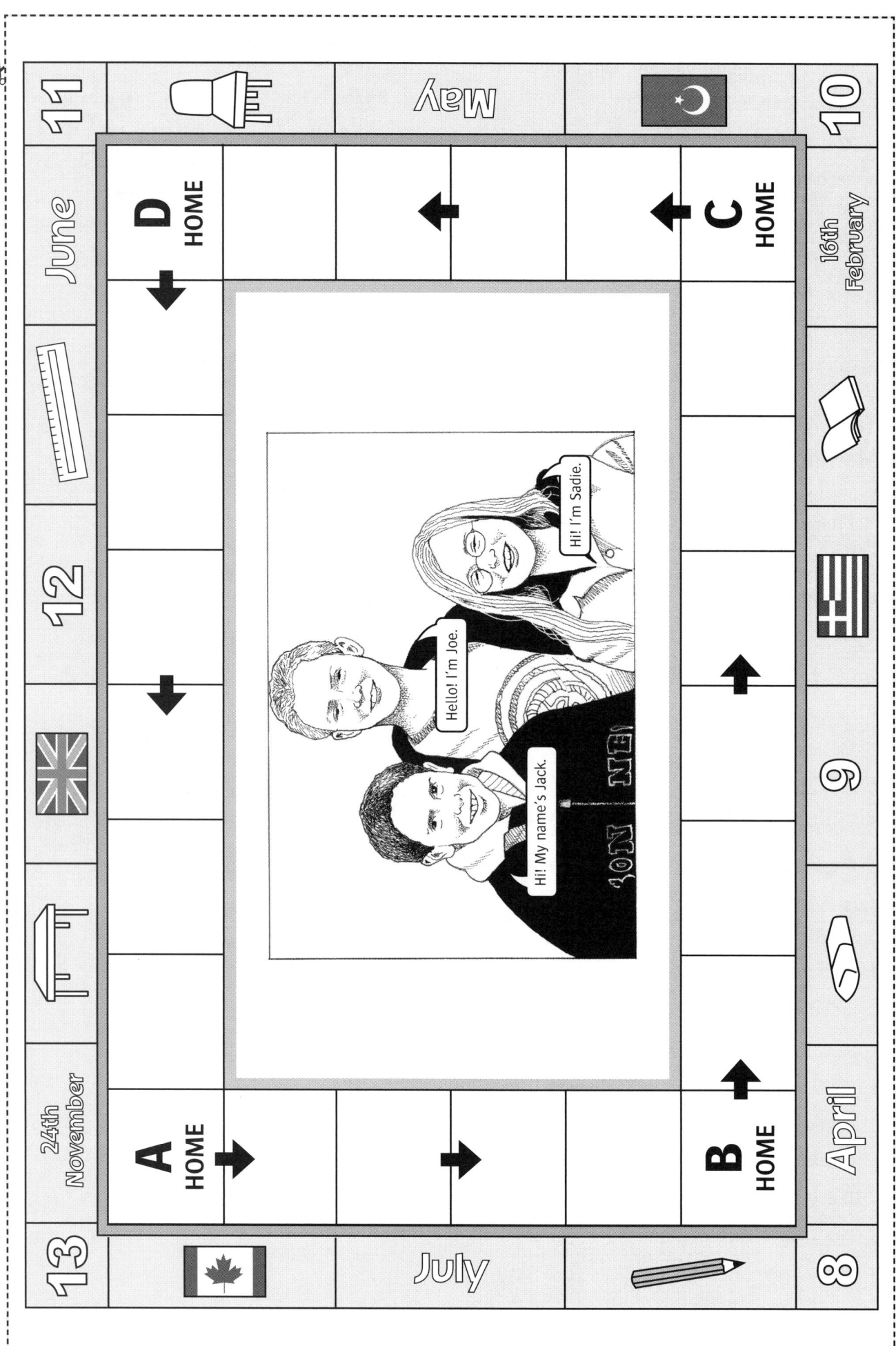

What's your name? (Move 1 square)	**How do you say 'Goodbye' in your language?** (Move 2 squares)
How are you? (Move 1 square)	**What nationality is Joe?** (Move 4 squares)
What nationality are you? (Move 3 squares)	**Find a thing beginning with *B* in the classroom.** (Move 2 squares)
How old are you? (Move 2 squares)	**What's the number before thirty?** (Move 3 squares)
How old is Sadie? (Move 3 squares)	**How do you spell 'window'?** (Move 3 squares)
How do you spell 'pencil'? (Move 2 squares)	**What's the month before January?** (Move 4 squares)
What's the date today? (Move 4 squares)	**What's the name of Sadie's dog?** (Move 2 squares)
How do you spell 'bottle'? (Move 3 squares)	**What's the date tomorrow?** (Move 4 squares)
How do you say 'dog' in your language? (Move 1 square)	**How do you spell your name?** (Move 2 squares)
What's the third month of the year? (Move 4 squares)	**Who lives at 20 Maple Road?** (Move 3 squares)
What's the number after eleven? (Move 2 squares)	**How old is Joe?** (Move 3 squares)
What's the month after June? (Move 3 squares)	**When is your birthday?** (Move 3 squares)
Who is Sadie's brother? (Move 2 squares)	**Find a thing beginning with *R* in the classroom.** (Move 2 squares)
How do you spell 'address'? (Move 3 squares)	**How do you say 'tortoise' in your language?** (Move 3 squares)

1 *be*: affirmative

Complete the sentences.

1 Sophie is fourteen. _____She's_____ good at art and science.

2 This is Robert. _____ a student at my school.

3 A: Where are Nick and Emma?

   B: _____ on the beach.

4 A: _____ a brilliant drummer, Sadie.

   B: Oh, thanks!

5 My name's Carlos and _____ from Spain.

6 The Mississippi isn't a mountain. _____ a river.

7 Sam and I are in Class 8B. _____ students at Lynford School.

8 Ellie is good at music and _____ interested in computers.

2 *Wh-* questions

Match the questions with the answers.

1	Who's Wayne Rooney?	a	9th May.
2	Where's Canberra?	b	At four o'clock.
3	What's the capital of the USA?	c	She's from France.
4	When's his birthday?	d	It's in Australia.
5	Who's the singer in the band?	e	Tennis.
6	Where's Annette from?	f	He's a footballer.
7	What's your favourite sport?	g	Mel.
8	When's your music class?	h	Washington.

1 _f_ 2 ____ 3 ____ 4 ____ 5 ____ 6 ____ 7 ____ 8 ____

3 *be*: negative

Complete the sentences. Use the negative form of *be*.

1 Kilimanjaro is in Africa but _____it isn't_____ a river.

2 They live in London but _____ English.

3 Anna is my friend but _____ in my class.

4 I like swimming but _____ interested in football.

5 Mike and Christine are students but _____ at Westover School.

6 Lee is in the band but _____ the leader.

7 Milan is in Italy but _____ the capital.

8 We're quite good at maths but _____ very good at science.

4 *be*: questions and short answers

Complete the questions and answers.

1 A: _____Are_____ Jack and Sadie friends?

   B: Yes, _____they are_____ .

2 A: _____ your sister good at geography?

   B: Yes, _____ .

3 A: _____ Alex your boyfriend?

   B: No, _____ .

4 A: _____ you a student?

   B: Yes, _____ .

5 A: _____ they interested in cars?

   B: No, _____ .

6 A: _____ Paris the capital of France?

   B: Yes, _____ .

7 A: _____ Sadie a keyboard player?

   B: No, _____ .

8 A: _____ you from Canada?

   B: No, _____ .

1 Is Washington a capital city?	13 Is Brazil in Europe?
2 Is Rome the capital of Italy?	14 Is Exeter in England?
3 Is Sydney the capital of Australia?	15 Are Jack and Annie cousins?
4 Is Paris a country?	16 Are Mark and Annie from England?
5 Are the Great Lakes in England?	17 Is Mountain the name of Joe's band?
6 Is France in Europe?	18 Is Mel a member of the band?
7 Are Barcelona and London cities?	19 Is Joe the drummer in the band?
8 Are the Andes mountains?	20 Is Jack good at science?
9 Is Argentina in Africa?	21 Are Lee and Barney guitarists?
10 Is the Mississippi a volcano?	22 Is Sadie from Australia?
11 Is Madrid the capital of Spain?	23 Are Sadie and Joe students?
12 Is the Thames in Washington?	24 Is Sam a student?

Answers: 1 Yes, it is. 2 Yes, it is. 3 No, it isn't. (Canberra is the capital of Australia.) 4 No, it isn't. (It's a city.) 5 No, they aren't. (They're in Canada and the USA.) 6 Yes, it is. 7 Yes, they are. 8 Yes, they are. 9 No, it isn't. (It's in South America.) 10 No, it isn't. (It's a river.) 11 Yes, it is. 12 No, it isn't. (It's in London.) 13 No, it isn't. (It's in South America.) 14 Yes, it is. 15 No, they aren't. (Sadie and Annie are cousins.) 16 No, they aren't. (They're from Australia.) 17 No, it isn't. (The name is Monsoon.) 18 Yes, she is. 19 No, he isn't. (He's the keyboard player. Sadie is the drummer.) 20 Yes, he is. 21 Yes, they are. 22 No, she isn't. (She's from England / Britain / the UK.) 23 Yes, they are. 24 No, he isn't. (He's a dog.)

1 a/an or some

Complete the sentences with *a, an* or *some*.

1 I've got ....*some*....... CDs in my room.

2 We've got .... sandwiches for lunch.

3 They've got .... umbrella.

4 Joe and Sadie have got .... dog called Sam.

5 You've got .... keys in your pocket.

6 They've got .... English dictionary.

7 Terry and Alan have got .... computer games.

8 I've got .... bike and .... skateboard.

2 have got + some/any

Make sentences. Use the right form of *have got* with *some* or *any*.

1 I / got / peanuts

I've got some peanuts.

2 They / got / books

....

3 you / got / crisps ?

....

4 We / not got / cousins

....

5 they / got / photos ?

....

6 I / not got / tissues

....

7 We / got / badges

....

8 They / not got / friends

....

3 Possessive 's

Complete the sentences. Use the possessive *'s*.

1 This is ....*Jack's*....... watch. (*Jack*)

2 I've got .... pencil case. (*Diana*)

3 .... lunchbox is in his bag. (*Lee*)

4 Where's .... bike? (*your friend*)

5 He's got .... umbrella. (*his father*)

6 What's .... name? (*your cat*)

7 She's .... grandmother. (*Bill and Clare*)

8 Where's .... house? (*your aunt and uncle*)

4 Possessive adjectives

Complete the sentences with possessive adjectives.

1 She's good at maths but ....*her*....... favourite subject is art.

2 I live with .... mother and father in London.

3 Mark is a student. .... school is in North Road.

4 We live in Exeter. .... address is 8 Turret Street.

5 I've got a sister. .... name's Emma and she's eight.

6 Alex and Caroline are in France with .... parents.

7 Emma, can I use .... calculator, please?

8 Tom is fifteen. It's .... birthday today.

Student A

1 Tell your partner about Greg.

What has he got

- in his bag?
- in his hand?
- in his lunchbox?

A: He's got a football in his bag.
   He's got some ...

Greg

2 What has Sarah got? Listen to your partner and draw her things in the picture.

3 Work with your partner. Look at your pictures and <u>underline</u> the right word(s) in each sentence.

1 (*Greg / Sarah*) has got football practice today.
2 (*Greg / Sarah*) is a tennis player.
3 (*Greg / Sarah*) hasn't got an umbrella.
4 Greg's keys (*are / aren't*) in his hand.
5 (*There's / There isn't*) a banana in Sarah's lunchbox.
6 There are some crisps in (*Greg's / Sarah's*) lunchbox.
7 Sarah (*has / hasn't*) got a mobile in her bag.

Sarah

Student B

1 What has Greg got? Listen to your partner and draw his things in the picture.

2 Tell your partner about Sarah.

What has she got

- in her bag?
- in her hand?
- in her lunchbox?

B: She's got a calculator in her bag.
   She's got some ...

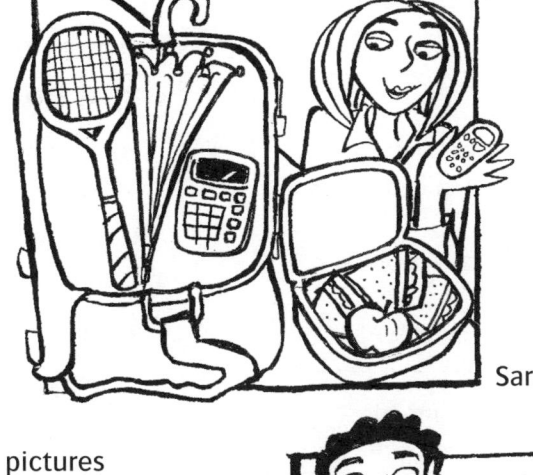

Sarah

3 Work with your partner. Look at your pictures and <u>underline</u> the right word(s) in each sentence.

1 (*Greg / Sarah*) has got football practice today.
2 (*Greg / Sarah*) is a tennis player.
3 (*Greg / Sarah*) hasn't got an umbrella.
4 Greg's keys (*are / aren't*) in his hand.
5 (*There's / There isn't*) a banana in Sarah's lunchbox.
6 There are some crisps in (*Greg's / Sarah's*) lunchbox.
7 Sarah (*has / hasn't*) got a mobile in her bag.

Greg

1 Position of adjectives

Complete the sentences.

1 The book is brilliant.

It's a _____ brilliant book _____ .

2 My hair is short.

I've got _____ .

3 That man is tall.

He's a _____ .

4 The dog isn't very friendly.

It isn't a _____ .

5 Their eyes are brown.

They've got _____ .

6 My surfboard is new.

It's a _____ .

7 These animals are dangerous.

They're _____ .

8 Lucy's hair is long and curly.

She's got _____ .

2 has/hasn't got

Look at the information and complete the sentences about Steve with has got or hasn't got.

Steve

Eyes:	blue
Hair:	short, straight, black
Brothers:	0
Sisters:	2 (Elizabeth and Jane)
Pets:	0
Personality:	kind, friendly

1 He _____ 's got _____ a friendly personality.

2 He _____ brown eyes.

3 He _____ a sister called Elizabeth.

4 He _____ long hair.

5 He _____ a dog.

6 He _____ dark hair.

7 He _____ straight hair.

8 He _____ any brothers.

3 have/has got: questions and short answers

Make questions with have got and complete the answers.

1 you / a mobile ?

A: Have you got a mobile?

B: No, _____ I haven't _____ .

2 she / a cold ?

A: _____

B: Yes, _____ .

3 Richard / a bike ?

A: _____

B: No, _____ .

4 you and Helen / any videos ?

A: _____

B: Yes, _____ .

5 your parents / a big car ?

A: _____

B: No, _____ .

6 horses / long legs ?

A: _____

B: Yes, _____ .

4 have/has got: affirmative, negative and questions

Find a mistake in each sentence. Underline the mistakes and correct them.

1 I'm got small eyes and a long nose. _____ I've _____

2 Linda got a bad headache. _____

3 Harry's parents has got an old computer. _____

4 Are you got a new watch? _____

5 Maria has got a cat but she not has got a dog. _____

6 Is Rebecca's boyfriend got dark hair? _____

7 The children isn't got any sandwiches. _____

8 Has Carl and Paul got any computer games? _____

Messages 1 `PHOTOCOPIABLE` © Cambridge University Press 2005 Module 2 resources Unit 4

Student A

1 Ask your partner to describe Sandra and Leo. Listen and complete your picture.

A: What's Sandra like?

2 Describe Terry and Joanna to your partner.

A: Terry's got short dark hair and ...

Terry   Sandra   Joanna   Leo

Student B

1 Describe Sandra and Leo to your partner.

B: Sandra's got small eyes and ...

2 Ask your partner to describe Terry and Joanna. Listen and complete your picture.

B: What's Terry like?

Terry   Sandra   Joanna   Leo

Messages 1   PHOTOCOPIABLE   © Cambridge University Press 2005   Module 2 resources Unit 4

RESOURCES UNIT 4   COMMUNICATION ACTIVITY

1 Present simple: affirmative

Complete the sentences. Use the right form of the verbs in the box.

live   wear   play   read   use   go   ~~drink~~ write

1 Dad _drinks_ coffee after lunch.

2 You _____ a lot of books.

3 We _____ in a small house in Liverpool.

4 Danny _____ to Westover School.

5 I _____ emails to my friends.

6 Emma's sister _____ the keyboard in a band.

7 Carl _____ a blue school uniform.

8 A lot of students _____ computers for their homework.

2 Present simple: affirmative and negative

Complete the sentences. Use the affirmative or negative form of the verbs.

1 I believe in ghosts but I _don't believe_ in vampires. (*believe*)

2 My brother is scared of dogs but he _____ cats. (*love*)

3 We don't play tennis but we _____ it on TV. (*watch*)

4 Tanya's a vegetarian. She _____ meat. (*eat*)

5 They use a computer but they _____ computer games. (*play*)

6 Cathy's very good at sport. She _____ to a sports club in North London. (*go*)

7 I _____ an apple. I really like fruit. (*want*)

8 Our teacher _____ from the USA. He's Australian. (*come*)

3 Present simple: questions and short answers

Complete the questions and answers.

1 A: _Do_ your friends _like_ music? (*like*)
  B: Yes, _they do_ .

2 A: _____ you _____ in UFOs? (*believe*)
  B: No, _____ .

3 A: _____ Maria _____ TV every day? (*watch*)
  B: Yes, _____ .

4 A: _____ your parents _____ a lot of books? (*read*)
  B: No, _____ .

5 A: _____ her grandfather _____ the piano? (*play*)
  B: Yes, _____ .

6 A: _____ Sandro _____ from France? (*come*)
  B: No, _____ .

7 A: _____ you both _____ a school uniform? (*wear*)
  B: No, _____ .

8 A: _____ bats _____ insects? (*eat*)
  B: Yes, _____ .

4 Wh- questions

Complete the questions.

1 A: _When_ 's your guitar lesson?
  B: At five o'clock.

2 A: _____ do you eat for lunch?
  B: Sandwiches and fruit.

3 A: _____ does Harry live?
  B: In New York.

4 A: _____ 's your birthday?
  B: In May.

5 A: _____ do you watch horror films?
  B: Because they're really exciting.

Student A

1 Take it in turns to ask and answer questions. Complete the table.

A: Does Robert play the guitar?   B: Yes, he does.

	play	use	read a lot	play	listen	eat meat	watch
Robert			✓	✗		✓	✓
Anna	✓	✗			✓	✓	✗
Andrew		✓	✗	✗		✓	
Laura	✗		✓		✓		✓

2 Work with your partner. Use the information in the table to complete the sentences.

1 _____Robert_____ and _____ don't play computer games at home.

2 _____ doesn't like music.

3 _____ has got lots of books and magazines.

4 _____ is very good at music.

5 _____ and _____ don't like books.

6 _____ is a vegetarian.

7 _____ and _____ listen to music but they don't write emails.

✂

Student B

1 Take it in turns to ask and answer questions. Complete the table.

A: Does Robert play the guitar?   B: Yes, he does.

	play	use	read a lot	play	listen	eat meat	watch
Robert	✓	✗			✓	✓	✓
Anna	✓	✗	✗	✓			
Andrew	✗		✗		✗	✓	✓
Laura		✓		✗	✓	✗	

2 Work with your partner. Use the information in the table to complete the sentences.

1 _____Robert_____ and _____ don't play computer games at home.

2 _____ doesn't like music.

3 _____ has got lots of books and magazines.

4 _____ is very good at music.

5 _____ and _____ don't like books.

6 _____ is a vegetarian.

7 _____ and _____ listen to music but they don't write emails.

1 Position of frequency adverbs

Put the words in the right order and make sentences.

1 eats / Andrew / fish / never

Andrew never eats fish.

2 often / my / I / tidy / room

3 drink / my / always / tea / parents

4 is / popular / usually / pasta

5 to / sometimes / the / catches / Joe / bus / school

6 always / are / dogs / energetic / your

7 is / lunchtime / at / Christine / hungry / usually

8 TV / James / in / never / evening / watches / the

2 Present simple and frequency

Find a mistake in each sentence. <u>Underline</u> the mistakes and correct them.

1 They <u>listen never</u> to the teacher.

never listen

2 Alice often is bored at school.

3 I go usually to the shop at lunchtime.

4 He always dos his homework before dinner.

5 My mother don't often eat meat.

6 We drink always water with our meal.

7 Ben sometimes haves eggs for breakfast.

8 They often are late.

3 Present simple and frequency

Make negative sentences. Put the adverb in the right position.

1 I / not eat / cheese. (*often*)

I don't often eat cheese.

2 Patrick / not watch / TV after school. (*always*)

3 She / not be / on time. (*usually*)

4 Giraffes / not attack / people. (*usually*)

5 We / not have /eggs for breakfast. (*usually*)

6 Michael and Greg / not be / late for school. (*often*)

4 Present simple: questions and short answers

Make questions. Then use the information in the boxes to write the answers.

Lisa		Robert	
7.40	get up	6.45	get up
7.45	shower	7.10	swimming pool
8.00	breakfast	7.50	shower / pool
8.25	leave home	8.00	home
8.30	catch bus	8.10	breakfast
8.40	get to school	8.30	catch bus
		8.40	get to school

1 When / Lisa / get up ?

When does Lisa get up? At 7.40.

2 Robert / get up / before Lisa ?

3 Where / Robert / have a shower ?

4 Lisa / have a shower / after breakfast ?

5 they / walk / to school?

6 What time / they / get to school?

Messages 1 PHOTOCOPIABLE © Cambridge University Press 2005 Module 3 resources Unit 6

Student A

1 Take it in turns to ask about the missing words in your puzzle and to describe the animals in your puzzle for your partner.

   A: What's 1 across?

   B: It's a big animal and it lives in the sea. It sometimes attacks people, but it usually eats fish.

2 Work with your partner. Complete the sentences with animals from the puzzle and verbs in the affirmative or negative.

   1 (*1 down*): A *snake hasn't* got any legs.

   2 (*3 down*): .... usually
   .... in groups.

   3 (*1 across*): A ....
   .... a type of fish.

   4 (*7 down*): ....
   other animals and then they eat them.

   5 (*6 across*): ....
   in the winter.

   6 (*9 across*): A .... never
   .... meat.

   7 (*3 across*): ....
   in Africa.

   8 (*8 across*): A ....
   .... a dangerous animal.

Crossword (Student A):

Row 1: ¹S H A R K
Down from S: N A K (SNAKE)
²(empty)
³G I R A F ⁴F E ⁵S (GIRAFFES)
⁶B E A R S (BEARS)
⁷(empty)
⁸D O L P H I N (DOLPHIN)
⁹(empty boxes)

Student B

1 Take it in turns to ask about the missing words in your puzzle and to describe the animals in your puzzle for your partner.

   A: What's 1 across?

   B: It's a big animal and it lives in the sea. It sometimes attacks people, but it usually eats fish.

2 Work with your partner. Complete the sentences with animals from the puzzle and verbs in the affirmative or negative.

   1 (*1 down*): A *snake hasn't* got any legs.

   2 (*3 down*): .... usually
   .... in groups.

   3 (*1 across*): A ....
   .... a type of fish.

   4 (*7 down*): ....
   other animals and then they eat them.

   5 (*6 across*): ....
   .... in the winter.

   6 (*9 across*): A .... never
   .... meat.

   7 (*3 across*): ....
   .... in Africa.

   8 (*8 across*): A ....
   .... a dangerous animal.

Crossword (Student B):

Row 1: ¹S H A R K
²C A T (CAT - down)
³G O R I L L A (GORILLA - down)
⁴(empty)
⁵S P I D E R S (SPIDERS - down)
⁶(empty)
⁷L I O N S (LIONS - down)
⁸(empty)
⁹H O R S E S (HORSES)

1 There is/are

Complete the sentences with *There's, There are, There isn't* or *There aren't*.

1 ✓ _____There are_____ some trees in the garden.

   ✗ _____There isn't_____ a telephone in the bedroom.

2 ✓ _____ a cinema next to our school.

3 ✗ _____ any tomatoes in the shop.

4 ✗ _____ any butter on the table.

5 ✓ _____ two bathrooms in Mary's house.

6 ✗ _____ any meat in this recipe.

7 ✗ _____ any cupboards in the apartment.

8 ✓ _____ a shower in the bathroom.

2 Is/Are there any ...? + short answers

Make questions and complete the answers.

1 onions / in the cupboard ?

   A: *Are there any onions in the cupboard?*

   B: Yes, _____there are_____ .

2 cheese / in the kitchen ?

   A: _____

   B: Yes, _____ .

3 books / in your bag ?

   A: _____

   B: No, _____ .

4 fruit juice / in the bottle ?

   A: _____

   B: No, _____ .

5 computers / at your school ?

   A: _____

   B: Yes, _____ .

6 paper / on your desk ?

   A: _____

   B: No, _____ .

7 shelves / in the wardrobe ?

   A: _____

   B: No, _____ .

8 bread / on the table ?

   A: _____

   B: Yes, _____ .

3 a, some or any?

Complete the sentences with *a, some* or *any*.

1 I want _____some_____ apple juice.

2 There are _____ videos downstairs.

3 There's _____ swimming pool in her garden.

4 We haven't got _____ mushrooms.

5 Have you got _____ bottle of water?

6 There isn't _____ cereal in the cupboard.

7 We need _____ tomatoes.

8 Is there _____ coffee in the kitchen?

4 There is/are + a, some or any

Match the words in A with the words in B and make sentences.

A	B
1 Is there a	a any students in the room.
2 There's some	b posters in your bedroom?
3 There isn't	c any meat in my sandwich.
4 Is there any	d CDs in the living room.
5 There aren't	e park in your town?
6 There are some	f window in the bathroom.
7 Are there any	g fruit on the table.
8 There isn't a	h bread in the cupboard?

1 _e_ 2 _____ 3 _____ 4 _____ 5 _____ 6 _____ 7 _____ 8 _____

Student A

Find seven differences between your picture and your partner's picture. Describe your picture to your partner. Begin:

A: In my picture there's a big table and there are three chairs.

Student B

Find seven differences between your picture and your partner's picture. Listen to Student A first. Then describe your picture.

B: Yes, in my picture there's a big table too, but there are two chairs, not three. So that's one difference.

RESOURCES UNIT 7   COMMUNICATION ACTIVITY

1 can/can't for ability

Match the questions (1–8) with the answers (a–h).

1 Can Helen play the guitar?
2 Can you speak French?
3 Can you draw?
4 Can horses fly?
5 Can you play football?
6 Can Lee cook?
7 Can cats see in the dark?
8 Can Tom play the piano?

a No, they can't. They haven't got wings.
b Yes, she can. She plays in a band.
c Yes, I can. I'm quite good at sport.
d No, he can't. He doesn't like music.
e No, we can't. Our pictures are awful!
f Yes, they can. They've got very good eyes.
g No, I can't. I'm not very good at languages.
h Yes, he can. He makes really nice pizzas.

1 __b__ 2 ___ 3 ___ 4 ___ 5 ___ 6 ___ 7 ___ 8 ___

2 can/can't for possibility

Complete the sentences. Use the verbs with can or can't.

1 You ___can hear___ music in a church. (hear)

2 You _____ lions at an aquarium. (see)

3 She _____ some new clothes at the shopping centre. (buy)

4 We _____ a train at the station. (catch)

5 People _____ bowling in a museum. (go)

6 You _____ skiing at a swimming pool. (go)

7 You _____ films at a cinema. (watch)

8 He _____ some exercise at the sports centre. (get)

3 must/mustn't

Write the sentences with must or mustn't.

1 Go home!
   __You must go home.__

2 Don't eat in class.
   _____

3 Don't argue!
   _____

4 Answer the question.
   _____

5 Help me!
   _____

6 Don't ride your bike here.
   _____

7 Practise the piano every day.
   _____

8 Don't be rude!
   _____

4 Imperative

Complete the instructions. Use the right form of the verbs in the box.

be	not be	listen	not listen	go	not go
get	not get				

1 She's silly. __Don't listen__ to Emily.

2 Go outside and _____ some exercise!

3 _____ quiet! We can't hear the music.

4 _____ swimming in that river. It's dangerous.

5 _____ any milk at the shop. We've got two bottles here.

6 _____ to bed now. It's late.

7 _____ late! You must be home at ten o'clock.

8 _____ to this song! It's really brilliant!

Messages 1 PHOTOCOPIABLE © Cambridge University Press 2005 Module 4 resources Unit 8

Student A

Take it in turns to ask about the missing places and complete your map. When your partner asks a question, describe the place without saying its name.

A: What's number 1?

B: It's a big building. You can go shopping there, and you can buy lots of different things.

A: A supermarket?

B: Yes, that's right.

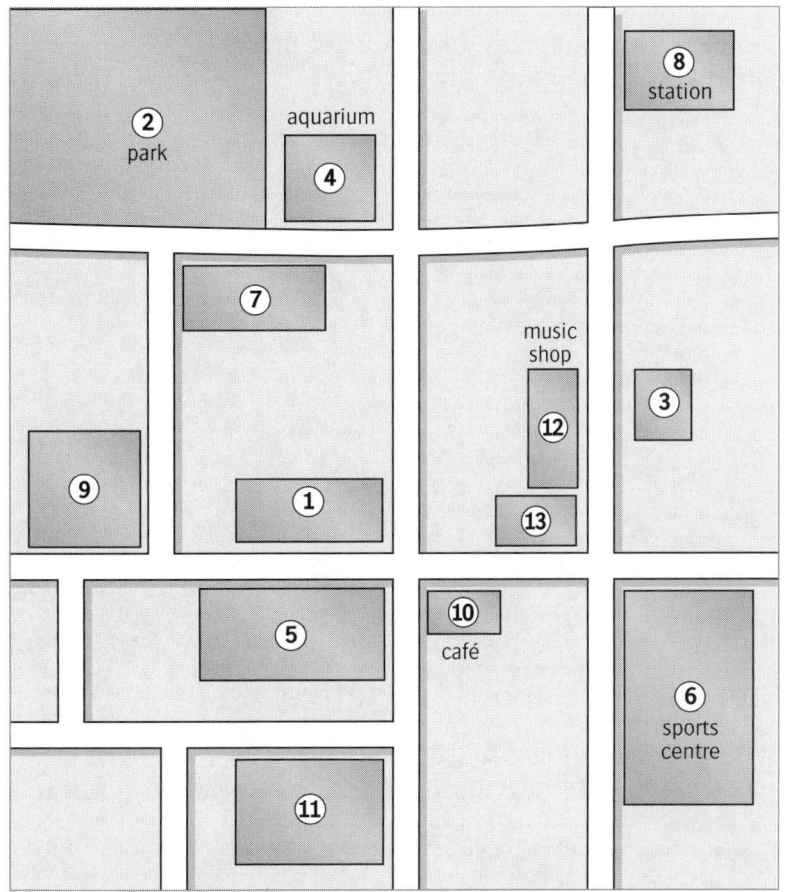

Student B

Take it in turns to ask about the missing places and complete your map. When your partner asks a question, describe the place without saying its name.

A: What's number 1?

B: It's a big building. You can go shopping there, and you can buy lots of different things.

A: A supermarket?

B: Yes, that's right.

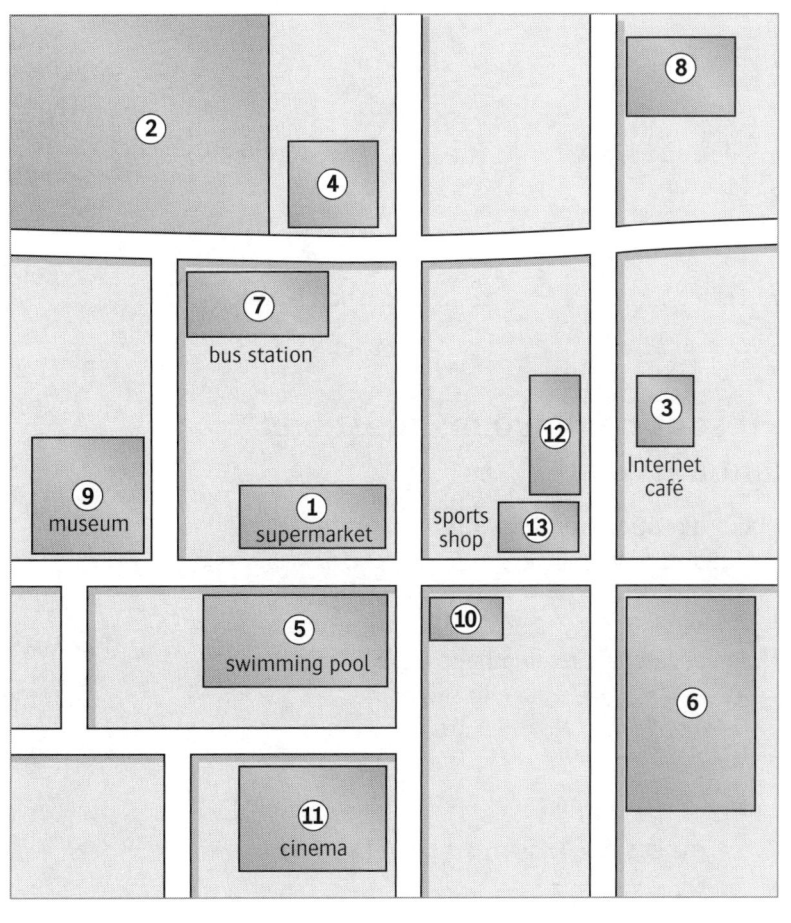

1 Present continuous: affirmative

Complete the sentences. Use the right present continuous form of the verbs.

1 Joe _____'s doing_____ a history test. (*do*)

2 She _____ a shower. (*have*)

3 I _____ trainers today. (*wear*)

4 We _____ Dad. (*help*)

5 The woman _____ out of the window. (*look*)

6 Mr and Mrs Kelly _____ in the garden. (*sit*)

7 David _____ in London at the moment. (*work*)

8 The children _____ . (*play*)

2 Present continuous: negative

Complete the sentences. Use the right negative form of the verbs in the box.

| read | ~~carry~~ | wear | listen | ride | watch |
| play | do |

1 Jane _____isn't carrying_____ a bag.

2 He _____ television.

3 We _____ gloves.

4 Nick and Jamie _____ football.

5 You _____ to me!

6 I _____ this magazine.

7 They _____ their homework.

8 She _____ her bike.

3 Present continuous: questions and answers

Make questions and match them with the answers in the box.

I'm cleaning my shoes.   No, they aren't.
Because she's feeling happy.   Yes, she is.
~~Yes, I am.~~   He's playing the piano.
In New York.   No, he isn't.

1 you / tidy / your room ?

A: *Are you tidying your room?*

B: *Yes, I am.*

2 he / write / an email ?

A: _____

B: _____

3 she / talk / to her boyfriend ?

A: _____

B: _____

4 What / you / do ?

A: _____

B: _____

5 Where / she / study ?

A: _____

B: _____

6 What / Jack / do ?

A: _____

B: _____

7 they / sit / on the beach ?

A: _____

B: _____

8 Why / Sadie / smile ?

A: _____

B: _____

4 Object pronouns

Complete the sentences with object pronouns.

1 Can you repeat that? I can't hear _____you_____ .

2 Robert's on the phone. Do you want to talk to _____ ?

3 This is a good film. We're really enjoying _____ .

4 I'm having problems with my homework. Can you help _____ ?

5 There are a lot of birds in the garden. I can see _____ from my window.

6 We're going swimming, but Liz doesn't want to come with _____ .

7 My aunt's in hospital. I must visit _____ this weekend.

8 Where are my glasses? I can't find _____ .

Messages 1 PHOTOCOPIABLE © Cambridge University Press 2005 Module 5 resources Unit 9

Student A

1 Ask your partner about these people: Sally, Steve, Tim, Liz and David.

   A: Who's Sally?

2 Answer your partner's questions about people in the picture.

   A: Luke's standing in front of the piano and he's wearing ...

3 There are now three people in the picture that you don't know. Read these sentences with your partner and work out who they are.

   Sarah never wears trousers. She doesn't like football. Beth can't play music but she loves football. Julie wears glasses.

Student B

1 Answer your partner's questions about people in the picture.

   B: Sally's sitting on a chair and she's wearing ...

2 Ask your partner about these people: Luke, John, Ann, Jenny and Robert.

   B: Who's Luke?

3 There are now three people in the picture that you don't know. Read these sentences with your partner and work out who they are.

   Sarah never wears trousers. She doesn't like football. Beth can't play music but she loves football. Julie wears glasses.

1 Present continuous used for the future

Complete the sentences. Use the right present continuous form of the verbs in the box.

come	have	catch	meet	go	play
not wear	not study				

1 Paula and Sue _are playing_ hockey next Tuesday.

2 We _____ Tony at 7.45 outside the cinema.

3 Rosa _____ to our house for lunch tomorrow.

4 I _____ the train at half past eleven.

5 Michael _____ French next year.

6 _____ you _____ to the dentist next week?

7 I _____ my new dress tomorrow.

8 _____ Danny _____ a party on Friday night?

2 Suggestions

Match the sentences in A with the suggestions in B.

A
1 It's cold.
2 It's her birthday.
3 It's hot.
4 I'm tired.
5 It's raining.
6 I'm hungry.
7 It's late.
8 I'm thirsty.

B
a Let's take an umbrella.
b Shall we have some orange juice?
c Why don't we close the window?
d Let's leave soon.
e Why don't we buy some crisps?
f Let's buy a present for her.
g Shall we go for a swim?
h Let's sit down for five minutes.

1 _c_ 2 ___ 3 ___ 4 ___ 5 ___ 6 ___ 7 ___ 8 ___

3 going to: affirmative and negative

Complete the sentences. Use the verbs with going to.

1 I _'m going to do_ my homework. (do)

2 They _____ some photos. (take)

3 Lee _____ a swim. (have)

4 We _____ the teacher. (ask)

5 Barney _____ visit the museum. (not visit)

6 I _____ basketball tomorrow. (not play)

7 She _____ her friend at the bowling alley. (meet)

8 My parents _____ TV this evening. (not watch)

4 going to: questions

Make questions and complete the answers.

1 they / catch / the bus ?
A: _Are they going to catch the bus?_
B: No, _they aren't_ .

2 Sharon / buy / a new tennis racket ?
A: _____
B: Yes, _____ .

3 Maria and Carlo / have / lunch with us ?
A: _____
B: No, _____ .

4 Andrew / walk / to school ?
A: _____
B: No, _____ .

5 your friends / come / to the party ?
A: _____
B: Yes, _____ .

6 you / fly / to Rome ?
A: _____
B: No, _____ .

Student A

1 Complete Mel's diary for next week. Ask your partner questions to find the missing information.

A: What time's Mel arriving at the museum on Monday morning?

B: At half past ten.

2 Now answer your partner's questions.

B: What time's Mel leaving the museum on Monday morning?

A: At twelve o'clock.

Mon	morning: museum – arrive __10.30__, leave 12.00	What time?
	_____ : tennis with Cathy	When?
Tues	before school: phone Barney	
	5.30: go to station – _____	Why?
Wed	Mum and Dad going to _____	Where?
	10.00: go to swimming pool	
	night: stay at Joe and Sadie's house	
Thurs	10.00: science test, _____	Where?
	4.00: practise with the band	
	evening: help _____ with posters for the concert	Who?
Fri	leave school 2.00 – dentist 2.45	
Sat	_____ – meet Sadie and Jack 11.30	Where?
	1.15: meet Helen for lunch	
	8.00: _____	What / do?
Sun	10.00: church	
	3.00: _____ on TV	What?
	8.00: cousins coming for dinner	

Student B

1 Look at Mel's diary and answer your partner's questions.

A: What time's Mel arriving at the museum on Monday morning?

B: At half past ten.

2 Complete Mel's diary for next week. Ask your partner questions to find the missing information.

B: What time's Mel leaving the museum on Monday morning?

A: At twelve o'clock.

Mon	morning: museum – arrive 10.30, leave __12.00__	What time?
	4.30: tennis with Cathy	
Tues	before school: phone _____	Who?
	5.30: go to station – meet David	
Wed	Mum and Dad going to London	
	10.00: go to _____	Where?
	_____ : stay at Joe and Sadie's house	When?
Thurs	10.00: science test, room 24	
	4.00: _____	What / do?
	evening: help Joe with posters for the concert	
Fri	leave school 2.00 – _____	Why?
Sat	market – meet Sadie and Jack 11.30	
	1.15: meet _____ for lunch	Who?
	8.00: cinema with John and Lucy	
Sun	10.00: _____	Where / go?
	3.00: football on TV	
	_____ : cousins coming for dinner	When?

1 was/were: affirmative and negative

Complete the sentences with *was, wasn't, were* or *weren't*.

1 The Beatles ___weren't___ painters. They were pop stars.

2 My cousins are American. They _____ born in New York.

3 The restaurant was quite nice, but the food _____ very interesting.

4 The snakes were big but they _____ dangerous.

5 I wasn't hungry, but I _____ very thirsty.

6 It _____ a windy morning but it wasn't cold.

7 The concert was great, Joe. You _____ fantastic!

8 Galileo _____ a footballer! He was a famous scientist.

2 was/were: questions and answers

Find a mistake in each sentence. Underline the mistakes and correct them.

1 Where you were this morning? ___were you___

2 I were at home. _____

3 Was they in the library? _____

4 Yes, they where. _____

5 When he's born? _____

6 He born in 1995. _____

7 She were a good singer. _____

8 No, she wasnt. _____

3 Past simple: affirmative

Complete the sentences. Use the past simple form of the verbs in the box.

| play   listen   study   ~~want~~   travel   carry |
| watch   tidy |

1 My aunt ___wanted___ to be an actress.

2 We _____ volleyball on the beach.

3 Joe and Sadie _____ a video in the evening.

4 He _____ history at university.

5 Steve _____ to the football match on the radio.

6 I _____ my room at the weekend.

7 Emma _____ her grandmother's bags to the station.

8 My family _____ to Germany in 2003.

4 Past simple: Wh- questions

Make questions and match them with the answers in the box.

A sports programme.	At half past ten.
Maths and science.	To find the station.
To Canada and the USA.	Her aunt and uncle.
In a supermarket.	~~On Saturday.~~

1 When / Peter / arrive ?
   A: *When did Peter arrive?*
   B: *On Saturday.*

2 Where / you / travel ?
   A: _____
   B: _____

3 Who / she / visit ?
   A: _____
   B: _____

4 What / they / watch / on TV ?
   A: _____
   B: _____

5 Where / she / work ?
   A: _____
   B: _____

6 What / they / study / at university ?
   A: _____
   B: _____

7 When / the concert / finish ?
   A: _____
   B: _____

8 What / those people / want ?
   A: _____
   B: _____

1 We watched a film at the cinema last night …

6 There were some CDs in the shop …

2 Yesterday morning it was cloudy …

7 Peter phoned Maria this morning …

3 There was a computer in Elizabeth's room …

8 We were thirsty …

4 Paula worked at a hotel last summer …

9 Caroline stayed in England last year …

5 Mike played football on Saturday …

…………… in the afternoon it started to rain.

…………… he didn't score a goal.

…………… she studied in London.

…………… she didn't like the job.

and then we walked home.

…………… we asked for some fruit juice.

…………… she used it to surf the Internet.

…………… they weren't very good.

…………… it wasn't cold.

…………… she didn't visit Scotland.

…………… Sam decided to buy one for his sister.

…………… she didn't want to speak to him.

but it wasn't very interesting.

…………… she saved a lot of money.

…………… his parents watched the match.

…………… it didn't belong to her.

…………… they talked for 20 minutes.

…………… there wasn't anything to drink.

1 Past simple: questions and short answers

Make questions and complete the short answers. Use the past simple.

1 your father / listen / to you ?

A: *Did your father listen to you?*

B: Yes, *he did* .

2 you / wait / outside the theatre ?

A: _____

B: No, _____ .

3 it / rain / last night ?

A: _____

B: No, _____ .

4 Karen / study / for the test ?

A: _____

B: Yes, _____ .

5 the children / help / with the housework ?

A: _____

B: No, _____ .

6 you and Ben / go swimming / yesterday ?

A: _____

B: Yes, _____ .

2 Past simple: affirmative and negative

Complete the sentences. Use the affirmative or negative form of the verbs.

1 Lisa cleaned the kitchen and *washed* the floor. (*wash*)

2 It was really cold this morning! I _____ to get up. (*want*)

3 I _____ to my teacher. She was very helpful. (*talk*)

4 The light was red but the car _____ . (*stop*)

5 Mark _____ every weekend and he saved a lot of money (*work*)

6 I tried to call Matthew but he _____ the phone. (*answer*)

3 Past simple: irregular verbs

Complete the sentences. Use the past simple form of the verbs in the box.

buy   know   go   ~~see~~   have   speak   leave eat

1 We _____ *saw* _____ some interesting pictures at the museum yesterday.

2 They _____ the library at 6.30 and walked home.

3 James _____ skiing in France last year.

4 Dad _____ some fruit and vegetables at the supermarket.

5 I _____ some orange juice and toast for breakfast.

6 You _____ my sandwiches!

7 My grandmother was brilliant. She _____ eight languages.

8 I _____ how to ride a horse when I was seven.

4 Irregular verbs: negative and questions

Find a mistake in each sentence. <u>Underline</u> the mistakes and correct them.

1 <u>Had you</u> lunch at the café?

Did you have

2 We not leave home on time yesterday.

_____

3 Joe not went swimming last week.

_____

4 Did they spoke English?

_____

5 I had a pen but I not had any paper.

_____

6 What you bought at the shop?

_____

7 It rained in the evening but it didn't was cold.

_____

8 When Jane came home?

_____

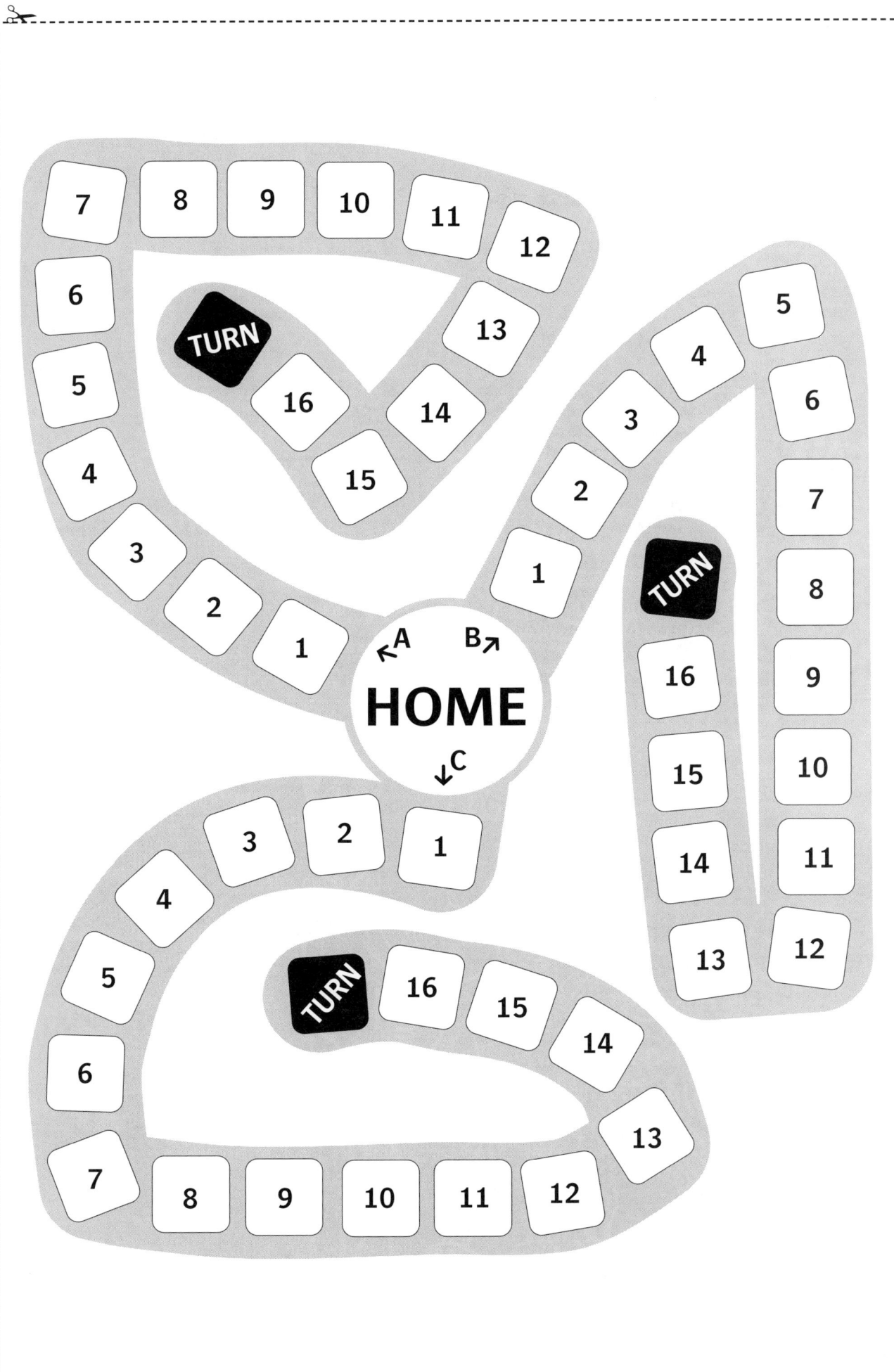

Student A questions

1 What's the weather like today?
2 What's your maths teacher's surname?
3 Say the names of three rooms in your home.
4 What's your teacher doing at the moment?
5 Was Marilyn Monroe a famous actress?
6 What are you going to watch on TV this evening?
7 What do people wear outside in the winter?
8 Who did Sadie and Lisa see at the concert? (Unit 12)
9 Where do people go bowling?
10 When did you arrive at school this morning?
11 Are you going to the cinema this evening?
12 Where do Sadie's cousins live? (Unit 2)
13 When's your birthday?
14 What was Sophie's gift from the cave in King's Hill? (Unit 12)
15 How many sisters has Joe got? (Unit 1)
16 What are you doing next weekend?

Student B questions

1 What's the third month of the year?
2 What subjects do you enjoy at school?
3 What does Mel do in the band? (Unit 2)
4 What's the time now?
5 What sport do people play on a *court*?
6 What did you have for breakfast this morning?
7 How many people are playing this game?
8 Who's Sadie's best friend? (Unit 3)
9 What football team does Lisa support? (Unit 9)
10 What are you doing in the summer holidays?
11 Where did Sophie go when she left King's Hill? (Unit 12)
12 Say the names of three types of buildings in your town.
13 Look at the person on your right. What is he/she wearing?
14 Did Christopher Columbus write music?
15 What are you going to do after school today?
16 What was Mr Neil's real name? (Unit 11)

Student C questions

1 What's the date today?
2 Who's sitting opposite you at the moment?
3 Say the names of three things you can drink.
4 Who helped the Pilgrim Fathers? (Unit 12)
5 What are you going to do after dinner this evening?
6 Can you ride a horse?
7 Where was Pablo Picasso born? (Unit 11)
8 When are you having your next class?
9 Who lives next door to Joe and Sadie? (Unit 1)
10 What sport do you watch at a *stadium*?
11 Did Jane Goodall study wild animals in Africa? (Unit 11)
12 When do you usually have dinner?
13 Who or what is called Lightning? (Unit 1)
14 What's your teacher wearing today?
15 Who lives on a houseboat? (Unit 7)
16 What did you have for lunch yesterday?

1 Grammar

a Complete the sentences. Circle the right answer: a, b or c.

0 I live .... Barcelona.

   a on   b at   ⓒ in

1 .... is Tokyo?

   a Who   b Where   c When

2 Italy and Spain are fantastic ....

   a countries   b country   c a country

3 ....'s the capital of France?

   a Who   b When   c What

4 ....'s your birthday?

   a What   b When   c Where

5 A: .... are you?

   B: I'm fine, thanks.

   a Where   b Who   c How

6 Vesuvius is ....

   a volcanoes   b volcano   c a volcano

7 My birthday's .... 1st April.

   a on   b at   c in

8 We are .... school.

   a on   b in   c at

9 .... I close the window, please?

   a Do   b Can   c Am

10 A: ....'s Mrs Smith?

    B: She's the English teacher.

   a Who   b When   c What

☐ 10

b Complete the sentences with the right form of *be*.

0 I '*m* .... twelve.

1 Where .... the Thames and the Mississippi?

2 A: Are you OK?

   B: Yes, I ....

3 Where .... your school?

4 Who .... Mark and Joe?

5 A: Is Rome in Spain?

   B: No, it ....

6 A: Are Paris and Calais in England?

   B: No, they ....

7 How old .... your cousins?

8 .... Dave English?

9 .... Sarah and Julia at home?

10 We .... English. We're Italian.

☐ 10

Grammar ☐ 20

MODULE 1 TEST

UNITS 1–2

2 Vocabulary

a Complete the sentences. Circle the right answer: a, b or c.

0 A: How are you?

B: ....

ⓐ All right, thanks.   b I'm James.   c He's fine.

1 My .... is Emma.

a surname   b name   c country

2 I'm good at ....

a England   b computer   c science

3 How do you .... 'school'?

a spell   b speak   c tell

4 London is a .... in England.

a river   b country   c city

5 Kilimanjaro is a .... in Africa.

a hill   b mountain   c lake

6 Can I .... your dictionary, please?

a look on   b look at   c look

7 Are you interested .... sport?

a in   b on   c at

8 Billy's the .... in the band.

a leading guitarist   b lead guitarist   c leading guitar

9 It's the second of March. Second = ...

a 2nd   b 3rd   c 1st

10 January, ... , March, April.

a July   b August   c February

| | 10 |

b What are these interests and activities? Put the letters in the right order and make words.

0 trosp   .... *sport* ....

1 tar	....	6 drangie	....
2 trompuce smage	....	7 gockoin	....
3 sminmiwg	....	8 blaftool	....
4 scuim	....	9 slamina	....
5 icsecen	....	10 cras	....

| | 10 |

| Vocabulary | 20 |

Read the text.

Name ....

Class .... Date ....

About me

Hello!

My name's Libby Johnson. I'm twelve years old and my birthday is on 14th November. I live with my mother, father and sister in Bournemouth, a town in the southwest of England. It's a nice town by the sea.

I'm a student at Highfields School. I'm good at science, geography and maths but I'm not good at art and sport. I'm interested in cooking, reading and swimming.

Now answer the questions.

0 What's her name?

Her name's Libby Johnson.

1 How old is she?

....

2 When's her birthday?

....

3 Where's Bournemouth?

....

4 What's Libby good at?

....

5 What's she interested in?

....

Reading	10

4 Writing

Read this letter from James.

Hi Emma,

My name's James and I'm thirteen years old. My birthday is on 1st January. I live in London with my family and my dog, Buster. I'm a student at Northgate School. I'm interested in geography and maths and I'm quite good at football and swimming. What about you?

Best wishes,

James

Write your answer to James. Write 25–35 words.

| Writing | 10 |

5 Listening

🔊 Listen to five students. For questions 1–5, write how they spell their names (for example: *P-A-U-L B-R-O-W-N*).

1 ....

2 ....

3 ....

4 ....

5 ....

🔊 Listen again and, for questions 6–10, write (in words) how old the students are (for example: *ten, twenty* etc).

6 ....

7 ....

8 ....

9 ....

10 ....

Listening	10
Speaking	10
Test total	80

MODULE 1 TEST   UNITS 1–2

Please note that the audio material for the Listening test is on the Class Cassettes/CD.

6 Speaking

a Two students answer your questions.

- Greet Students A and B and ask them how they are.

- Ask each student questions that you might ask when meeting people for the first time, to obtain information of a factual, personal kind, for example, about their name, age, family, school etc.

b Two students talk to each other.

- Give each student a copy of a prompt card (A or B) and explain that Student A should ask Student B for the information on the card. Student A should ask for the spelling of Student B's name and address and write them down. Student A should then repeat the spelling back.

- Student B should then ask Student A for the same information, asking for the spelling of their name and address, and repeating the spelling afterwards.

- Focus on their use of the correct question forms.

A Ask and answer questions.

Name: ....

Address: ....

....

Telephone number: ....

Age: ....

Birthday: ....

Interests: ....

B Ask and answer questions.

Name: ....

Address: ....

....

Telephone number: ....

Age: ....

Birthday: ....

Interests: ....

1 Grammar

a 1 b 2 a 3 c 4 b 5 c 6 c 7 a 8 c 9 b 10 a

b 1 are 2 am 3 's/is 4 are 5 isn't / 's not 6 aren't / 're not 7 are 8 Is
9 Are 10 aren't / 're not

2 Vocabulary

a 1 b 2 c 3 a 4 c 5 b 6 b 7 a 8 b 9 a 10 c

b 1 art 2 computer games 3 swimming 4 music 5 science 6 reading 7 cooking
8 football 9 animals 10 cars

3 Reading

1 She's twelve (years old).

2 (Her birthday's / It's) on 14th November / the fourteenth of November.

3 (Bournemouth's / It's) in the southwest of England.

4 (She's good at) science, geography and maths.

5 (She's interested in) cooking, reading and swimming.

4 Writing

Check individual answers.

5 Listening

Tapescript

1 A: What's your name?
   B: Chloe Reynolds.
   A: How do you spell that?
   B: C-H-L-O-E R-E-Y-N-O-L-D-S.
   A: Thank you. And how old are you, Chloe?
   B: I'm eleven.

2 A: What's your name?
   B: Lauren Matthews.
   A: How do you spell that?
   B: L-A-U-R-E-N M-A double T-H-E-W-S.
   A: Thank you. And how old are you, Lauren?
   B: I'm thirteen.

3 A: What's your name?
   B: George Waterman.
   A: How do you spell that?
   B: G-E-O-R-G-E W-A-T-E-R-M-A-N.
   A: Thank you. And how old are you, George?
   B: I'm twelve.

4 A: What's your name?
   B: Steven Ackerman.
   A: How do you spell that?
   B: S-T-E-V-E-N A-C-K-E-R-M-A-N.
   A: Thank you. And how old are you, Steven?
   B: I'm fifteen.

5 A: What's your name?
   B: Charlotte Jenkins.
   A: How do you spell that?
   B: C-H-A-R-L-O-T-T-E J-E-N-K-I-N-S.
   A: Thank you. And how old are you, Charlotte?
   B: I'm fourteen.

1 Chloe Reynolds 2 Lauren Matthews
3 George Waterman 4 Steven Ackerman
5 Charlotte Jenkins 6 eleven 7 thirteen
8 twelve 9 fifteen 10 fourteen

6 Speaking

Check individual answers.

1 Grammar

Name _____

Class _____ Date _____

a Complete the sentences. Circle the right answer: a, b or c.

0 My .... eyes are blue.

   a mothers'   (b) mother's   c mothers

1 I've got two sisters. .... names are Becky and Gemma.

   a Her   b Their   c Our

2 Have you got .... tissues?

   a some   b an   c any

3 A: I've got a new English teacher.

   B: .... ?

   a What are they like?   b What's she like?

   c What's she likes?

4 .... is a photo of my dog Judy.

   a This   b Those   c These

5 My .... got long, fair hair.

   a friend   b friend's   c friends

6 I've got a big, new pencil case. .... old pencil case is very small.

   a Our   b My   c Your

7 We've got an English lesson today with .... new English teacher.

   a their   b his   c our

8 Look! Is .... your brother?

   a those   b these   c that

9 A: What are your cousins like?

   B: ....

   a They're great.   b It's great.   c She's great.

10 .... got a dog?

   a Has you   b Have he   c Have you

   | 10 |

b Complete the sentences with *a, an, some* or *any*.

0 I've got _____ *an* _____ exciting computer game.

1 I haven't got _____ trainers.

2 Have you got _____ crisps?

3 Our teacher's got _____ new dictionaries.

4 Have you got _____ mobile phone?

5 I haven't got _____ anorak.

6 Have you got _____ calculator?

7 Beth's got _____ tissues in her bag.

8 We've got _____ English lesson today.

9 Has Jack got _____ new CDs?

10 I haven't got _____ baseball cap.

| | 10 |
| Grammar | 20 |

2 Vocabulary

a Complete the sentences. Circle the right answers: a, b or c.

0   My .... are tired!

   a foot   ⓑ feet   c foots

1   A: How are you?

   B: I'm fed ....

   a out   b on   c up

2   What's .... ?

   a the matter   b matter   c a matter

3   My mother's sister is my ....

   a cousin   b uncle   c aunt

4   Come on! Hurry .... !

   a up   b on   c in

5   My father's daughter is my ....

   a cousin   b aunt   c sister

6   I've got 32 ....

   a teeth   b tooth   c tooths

7   A: How are you?

   B: I've got ....

   a cold   b a cold   c the cold

8   Has John got .... ?

   a dark hairs   b the dark hair   c dark hair

9   My grandparents have got two .... – my mum and my uncle.

   a children   b sons   c daughters

10   Everyone is scared of Mr Black's dog. It's ....

   a friendly   b dangerous   c honest

b Label the parts of the body.

                                                              10

0   *head*

1   ....

2   ....

3   ....

4   ....

5   ....

6   ....

7   ....

8   ....

9   ....

10   ....

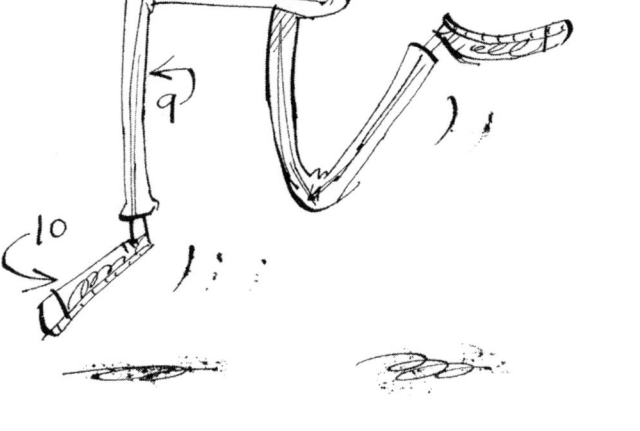

                                           10

Vocabulary	20

3 Reading

Read the text.

My family

My name's Jennifer and I'm fourteen years old. I'm quite quiet and serious. I live in Vancouver, Canada, with my parents, my brother Kevin and my two sisters Colleen and Sandra – oh yes, and we've got a funny dog called Rex.

My father, Ken, is a maths teacher. He's tall with fair hair and blue eyes. He's interesting and he's very funny. My mother, Kate, is also a teacher at my school. She's 38 and she's friendly and very kind.

My brother is interested in sport, sport and sport but my sisters aren't. They're good at science and maths. They're great sisters and they're my best friends. I've also got four uncles, four aunts and twelve cousins. We all live in Vancouver. Our birthdays are very noisy because we've got a big family!

Now answer the questions.

0   How old is Jennifer?

 She's fourteen years old.

1   How many brothers and sisters has she got?

....

2   What's the dog's name?

....

3   What's her father like?

....

....

4   How old is her mother?

....

5   Where's her mother a teacher?

....

6   What's Kevin interested in?

....

7   What are Colleen and Sandra like?

....

....

8   How many uncles has Jennifer got?

....

9   How many cousins has Jennifer got?

....

10   What are their birthdays like?

....

| Reading | 10 |

Messages 1   PHOTOCOPIABLE   © Cambridge University Press 2005   Module 2 test

4 Writing

Read this description of Dan.

> My brother, Dan, is twenty years old and he's a student.
> He's very tall and he's got dark, curly hair and big blue eyes.
> He's got a friendly face and he's a kind, honest person.

Now write a description of a friend or someone in your family. Write 25–35 words.

Writing	10

5 Listening

🔊 Listen to these five people speaking about their favourite things.
For questions 1–5, circle the right answer: a, b or c.

What is each speaker describing?

1
a   a favourite place
b   a favourite possession
c   a favourite person

2
a   a favourite city
b   a favourite person
c   a favourite place

3
a   a favourite TV programme
b   a favourite person
c   a favourite city

4
a   a favourite TV programme
b   a favourite place
c   a favourite possession

5
a   a favourite person
b   a favourite TV programme
c   a favourite city

🔊 Now listen again and, for questions 6–10, complete the sentences.

6   Speaker One's mobile phone is .... and silver.

7   Speaker Two's got a fantastic ....

8   Anne's got .... hair.

9   *This Is My House* is really ....

10 Sydney's got fantastic ....

Listening	10
Speaking	10
Test total	80

Please note that the audio material for the Listening test is on the Class Cassettes/CD.

Messages 1 PHOTOCOPIABLE © Cambridge University Press 2005 Module 2 test

6 Speaking

a Two students answer your questions.

- Greet Students A and B and ask them how they are.

- Ask each student questions about school, to obtain information of a factual, personal kind, for example, *What's your class like? What's your favourite subject?*.

b Two students talk to each other.

- Give Student A a copy of card 1A and give Student B a copy of card 1B. Explain that Student A should ask Student B to describe the pictures on their card.

- Give Student B a copy of card 2B and give Student A a copy of card 2A and this time Student B should ask Student A to describe what's on their card.

- Focus on the language of description and encourage the students to use as much vocabulary as possible.

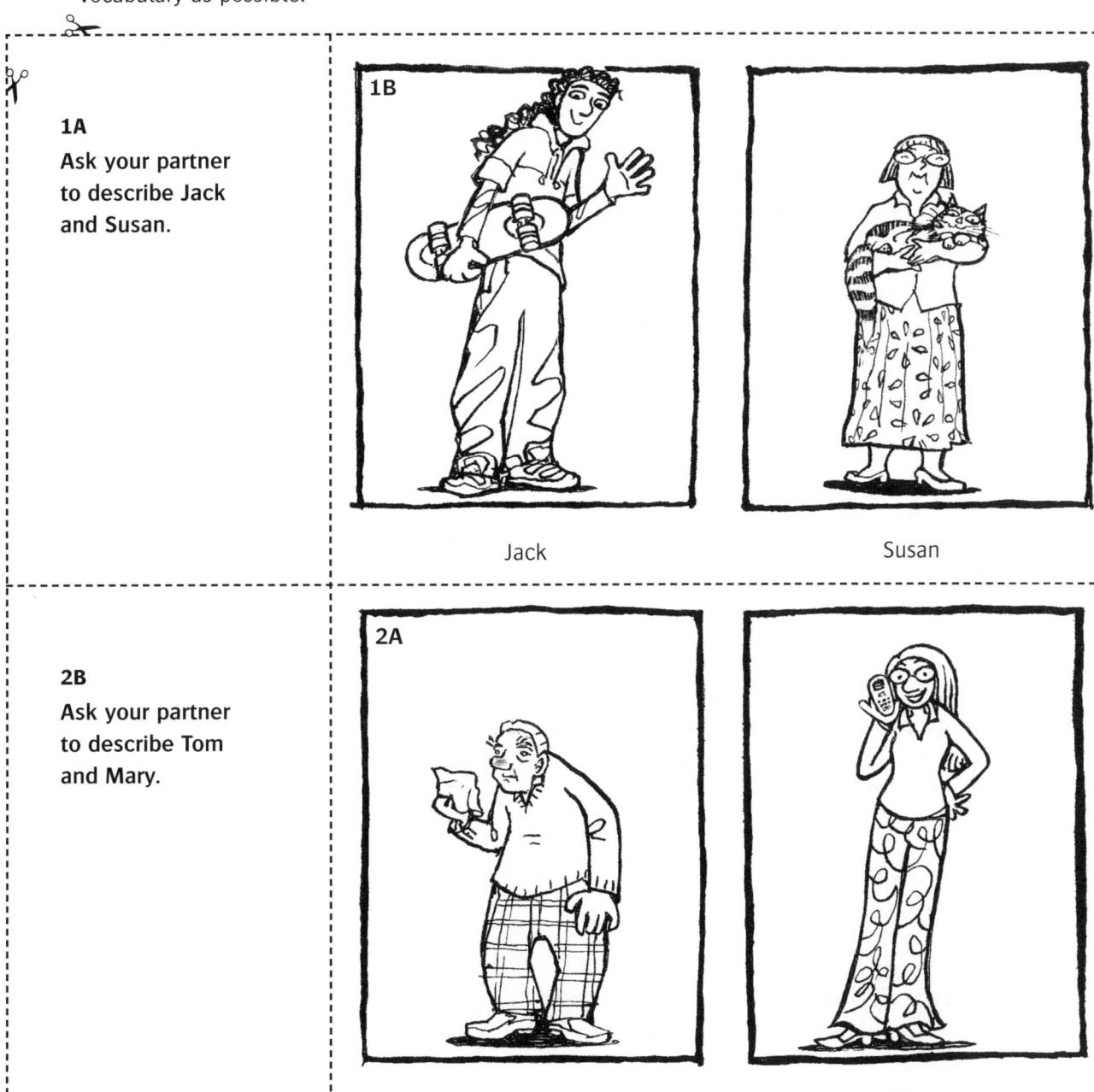

1A
Ask your partner to describe Jack and Susan.

1B

Jack   Susan

2B
Ask your partner to describe Tom and Mary.

2A

Tom   Mary

1 Grammar

a 1 b 2 c 3 b 4 a 5 b 6 b 7 c 8 c 9 a 10 c

b 1 any 2 any 3 some 4 a 5 an 6 a 7 some 8 an 9 any 10 a

2 Vocabulary

a 1 c 2 a 3 c 4 a 5 c 6 a 7 b 8 c 9 a 10 b

b 1 nose 2 face 3 mouth 4 ear 5 hair 6 eye 7 arm 8 hand 9 leg 10 foot

3 Reading

1 (She's got) one brother and two sisters.

2 (The dog's name is) Rex.

3 (Her father's / He's) tall with fair hair and blue eyes. He's interesting and very funny.

4 (Her mother's / She's) 38 (years old).

5 (Her mother's / She's a teacher) at her school.

6 (Kevin's/He's interested in) sport.

7 (Colleen and Sandra are / They're) good at science and maths and they're great sisters.

8 (She's got) four uncles.

9 (She's got) twelve cousins.

10 (Their birthdays are) very noisy.

4 Writing

Check individual answers.

5 Listening

Tapescript

1 My favourite thing is … my mobile phone. It's very small and it's blue and silver.
2 My grandparents have got a big, old house near the sea and I've got a fantastic room there.
3 Anne's my best friend. She's got straight hair and green eyes. She's friendly and funny.
4 My favourite TV programme is called *This Is My House*. It's **really great**! The houses are very interesting: big, small, old and new.
5 Sydney is a brilliant place! It's got fantastic beaches. It's a big, exciting city, but very friendly.

1 b 2 c 3 b 4 a 5 c 6 blue 7 room 8 straight 9 great 10 beaches

6 Speaking

Check individual answers.

1 Grammar

a Complete the sentences. Circle the right answer: a, b or c.

0 Kieran .... football.

(a) doesn't play   b don't play   c doesn't plays

1 Lucy always .... a shower in the morning.

a has got   b has   c have

2 When .... you do your homework?

a does   b are   c do

3 .... your brothers play football?

a Does   b Do   c Are

4 Michael .... always late for school.

a is   b comes   c goes

5 A: Do you like music?

B: Yes, ...

a I do   b I am   c I does

6 Sally .... TV every day.

a don't watch   b watch   c watches

7 .... reads comics after supper.

a I   b He   c They

8 Liam and Daniel .... live in London.

a aren't   b doesn't   c don't

9 We .... a computer at home.

a haven't got   b hasn't got   c don't got

10 My sister's birthday is .... January.

a on   b in   c at

| 10 |

b Complete the sentences with the right form of the verbs in the box.

| ~~live~~   eat   come   get up   not speak   read   drink   not like   help   go   tidy |

0 ____Do____ you ____live____ in Barcelona?

1 Kate _____ _____ English tests.

2 Where _____ you _____ from?

3 _____ you _____ comics?

4 James never _____ meat because he's a vegetarian.

5 I always _____ two litres of water a day.

6 _____ Steve _____ his father with the housework?

7 When _____ you _____ in the morning?

8 Sophie is very lazy. She never _____ her room.

9 John _____ to school by bus.

10 Sam and Rachel _____ _____ French or German.

| 10 |

| Grammar | 20 |

MODULE 3 TEST   UNITS 5–6

2 Vocabulary

a Label the pictures.

0 *chips* 1 .... 2 ....

3 .... 4 .... 5 ....

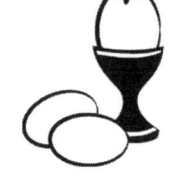

6 .... 7 .... 8 ....

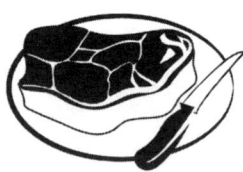

9 .... 10 ....

[ ] 10

b Circle the odd one out in each group.

0 breakfast   dinner   lunch   (bread)

1 spiders   ghosts   the dark   hair

2 town   city   volcano   capital

3 geography   tennis   volleyball   football

4 drummer   guitarist   teacher   keyboard player

5 socks   lunchbox   trainers   anorak

6 leg   ear   eye   nose

7 mother   father   brother   student

8 history   maths   computer games   science

9 nice   awful   good   great

10 coffee   milk   orange juice   curry

[ ] 10

| Vocabulary | 20 |

3 Reading

Read the text.

My name is Megan. I don't eat meat, but I eat fish, cheese and eggs. For breakfast I usually have a glass of milk and some fruit. At lunchtime I have my packed lunch – a cheese sandwich, a yoghurt and orange juice. I don't eat school meals because I don't like them. When I get home from school I usually have a snack – a packet of crisps or some fruit. For dinner we often have fish with salad or pasta.

My favourite meal is pizza. I sometimes go to a restaurant with my parents at the weekend. I love Italian food but my parents prefer French food so sometimes we have a pizza and sometimes we go to my parents' favourite restaurant. They always have steak and chips! It's difficult for me because I don't like meat, so I usually have salad!

I think good food is very important. I eat fruit and vegetables every day. My best friend never eats salad or fruit. She prefers burgers and sausages.

Sport is also very important. I play hockey every week and I always walk to school. I also go to a judo club on Wednesday with my sister Jenny.

Are these sentences true (T) or false (F)? Tick (✓) the right answer.

0	Megan eats meat.	T	F ✓
1	Megan doesn't eat cheese.	T	F ....
2	She always has milk and fruit for breakfast.	T	F ....
3	She doesn't have a school lunch.	T	F ....
4	She likes the school meals.	T	F ....
5	After school she usually has a snack.	T	F ....
6	Megan's favourite food is Italian.	T	F ....
7	Her parents' favourite restaurant is French.	T	F ....
8	Megan's best friend also eats fruit and vegetables.	T	F ....
9	Megan doesn't usually walk to school.	T	F ....
10	She goes to a judo club with her sister.	T	F ....

Reading   10

4 Writing

Read this email from Josh.

Hi Paolo,
What do you usually do at the weekend? I often play football and I always eat a lot of food! What time do you get up on Sunday? When do you do your homework?
Please write to me.
Josh

Write an email to Josh. Answer his questions. Write 25–35 words.

| Writing | 10 |

5 Listening

🔊 Listen to Anna and Mark talking about their likes and dislikes.
For questions 1–5, circle the right answer: a, b or c.

1 Mark is terrified of ....

   a bats   b rats   c cats

2 Anna thinks horror films are ....

   a exciting   b interesting   c bad

3 Anna doesn't like ....

   a thunder   b heights   c sharks

4 Mark's .... has got a rat.

   a mother   b father   c brother

5 Mark likes ....

   a English   b history   c hockey

🔊 Now listen again and, for questions 6–10, complete the sentences.

Mark is not scared of 6........................ .

Mark likes 7........................ , history and his 8........................ .

Anna likes 9........................ , music and 10........................ .

Listening	10
Speaking	10
Test total	80

Please note that the audio material for the Listening test is on the Class Cassettes/CD.

MODULE 3 TEST   UNITS 5–6

6 Speaking

a Two students answer your questions.

- Greet Students A and B and ask them how they are.

- Ask each student questions to obtain information of a personal kind, for example, about their habits, brothers/sisters, school, likes/dislikes etc.

b Two students talk to each other.

- Give Student A a copy of card 1A and give Student B a copy of card 1B. Explain that Student A should ask Student B questions, using the word prompts on the card. Student B should answer these questions using their prompts.

- Give Student A a copy of card 2A and give Student B a copy of card 2B. Explain that Student B should ask Student A questions about when they do certain things during the day. Student A should answer these questions using the prompts on the card.

1A   Ask your partner questions.

Do you often ...?

- play football
- go / cinema
- write emails
- help / home
- study English

a/w MT3.14

1B   Answer your partner's questions.

- football   – never
- cinema   – Saturday
- emails   – every day
- at home   – weekend
- English   – Monday/Wednesday/Friday

2A   Answer your partner's questions.

- do / homework – after school
- get up   – 6.30
- go / school   – 7.30
- have dinner   – 6.45
- go / bed   – 10.15

2B   Ask your partner questions.

When ...?

- do / homework
- get up
- go / school
- have dinner
- go / bed

1 Grammar

a 1 b 2 c 3 b 4 a 5 a 6 c 7 b 8 c 9 a 10 b

b 1 doesn't like 2 do, come 3 Do, read 4 eats 5 drink 6 Does, help 7 do, get up
  8 tidies 9 goes 10 don't speak

2 Vocabulary

a 1 sausages 2 cheese 3 bread 4 fish 5 sandwich 6 salad 7 eggs 8 fruit
  9 meat 10 vegetables

b 1 hair 2 volcano 3 geography 4 teacher 5 lunchbox 6 leg 7 student
  8 computer games 9 awful 10 curry

3 Reading

1 F 2 F 3 T 4 F 5 T 6 T 7 T 8 F 9 F 10 T

4 Writing

Check individual answers.

5 Listening

Tapescript

ANNA: I'm really scared of the dark because our house is very big and very old.

MARK: Are you? I'm not, but I'm terrified of bats!

ANNA: Because you watch those awful horror films every evening.

MARK: No, I don't. But I know you don't like thunder.

ANNA: That's right. I'm really scared of thunder. What about heights, then?

MARK: I'm not scared of heights!

ANNA: Rats?

MARK: Ah yes. I really don't like rats. They're awful! My brother's got a rat at home. Its name is Eric.

ANNA: So what do you like then?

MARK: I like comics, history and my computer. And you, Anna? What do you like?

ANNA: I like animals and music, and I really like sport. Anyway, it's time to do my homework.

1 a 2 c 3 a 4 c 5 b 6 heights 7 comics 8 computer 9 animals 10 sport

6 Speaking

Check individual answers.

1 Grammar

Name _____

Class _____ Date _____

a Complete the sentences. Circle the right answer: a, b or c.

0 You .... go to bed late tonight, because it's the weekend.

a don't ⓑ can c mustn't

1 My bed is .... of my bedroom.

a on the corner   b at the corner   c in the corner

2 .... rude to me. I don't like it.

a Don't be   b Be   c Not be

3 .... any vegetables in the kitchen.

a There are   b There aren't   c There isn't

4 Look at that man .... you.

a on the left   b on the right   c in front of

5 A: Where's the cat?

B: I think he's .... the bed again!

a above   b opposite   c under

6 Are there any mountains in England?

a No, there aren't.   b Yes, they are.

c No, there isn't.

7 .... some pasta in the cupboard.

a There are   b There's   c There isn't

8 I .... do my homework now. We've got a test tomorrow.

a must   b mustn't   c can't

9 Mr and Mrs Evans are in .... garden.

a they're   b their   c there

10 Would you like .... egg for breakfast?

a an   b a   c any

[10]

b Complete the sentences with *there's, there are, there isn't, there aren't, are there* or *is there.*

0 _____Is there_____ a swimming pool near your school?

1 _____ any good films at the cinema this week.

2 A: Is there any milk? I'm very thirsty.

B: No, _____ .

3 _____ a new gym in the sports centre.

4 _____ any good shops in town?

5 I'm sorry, _____ any bread.

6 A: _____ a cathedral in Salisbury?

B: Yes, there is.

7 _____ any tennis courts near here.

8 _____ two new shopping centres in the city.

9 A: Are there any boys in your class?

B: Yes, _____ .

10 _____ any ice cream.

[10]

| Grammar | 20 |

2 Vocabulary

a Label the furniture in the bedroom.

0 ___bed___

1 ....

2 ....

3 ....

4 ....

5 ....

6 ....

7 ....

8 ....

9 ....

10 ....

| | 10 |

b Complete the names of the places.

0 You can look at the fish at an a q u a r i u m.

1 You can surf the Internet at an I _ _ _ _ _ _ _ c _ _ _ .

2 You can go bowling at a b _ _ _ _ _ _ a _ _ _ _ .

3 You can play football or volleyball at a s _ _ _ _ _ c _ _ _ _ _ _ .

4 You can go for a walk in a p _ _ _ .

5 You can go swimming in a s _ _ _ _ _ _ _ p _ _ _ .

6 You can go shopping in a s _ _ _ _ _ _ _ c _ _ _ _ _ .

7 You can buy fruit, vegetables and meat at a s _ _ _ _ _ _ _ _ _ _ .

8 You can watch a film at a c _ _ _ _ _ _ .

9 You can play tennis on a t _ _ _ _ _ c _ _ _ _ .

10 You can look at old things in a m _ _ _ _ _ _ .

| | 10 |
| Vocabulary | 20 |

3 Reading

Read the text.

Sam is from England, but he lives in Prague, the capital of the Czech Republic. His parents are both English doctors and they work in a large hospital. Sam loves Prague because it's an interesting, exciting city. He goes to the International School where his lessons are in English, but he wants to learn Czech because he's got some Czech friends.

Sam and his parents live in a flat in the old part of Prague. It's got six rooms: two bedrooms, a living room, a dining room, a kitchen and a bathroom. It's on the third floor and Jack's got a fantastic view from his bedroom window. He can see the famous St. Vitus cathedral, the Vltava river and wonderful old streets with all their shops, bars and restaurants.

Prague is a great city for tourists because there are so many interesting things to do. You can go to a classical concert in a church. You can go shopping. You can surf the Net in an Internet Café. You can go to a museum and learn about the history of the Czech Republic. You can watch people in a street café. You can walk in the parks. You can go on the river. Or you can take a bus or a train to another town.

Now make questions for these answers.

0   *Where's Sam from?*

He's from England.

1   ....

He lives in Prague.

2   ....

In the Czech Republic.

3   ....

In a large hospital.

4   ....

Because he's got some Czech friends.

5   ....

Six.

6   ....

St. Vitus cathedral and the Vltava river.

7   ....

A church.

8   ....

In a museum.

9   ....

You can watch people.

10   ....

In the parks.

Reading | 10

4 Writing

Read this description of a kitchen.

Our kitchen is very big and light. There are three windows and you can see the park because we live on the tenth floor. There's a large table with ten chairs. We always eat in the kitchen because it's our favourite room. I've got five brothers and sisters so meal times are very noisy!

Now write a description of your favourite room. Write 25–35 words.

Writing		10

5 Listening

🔊 Listen to five people talking about their favourite rooms.
For questions 1–5, write the name of the room they are describing.

1 _____

2 _____

3 _____

4 _____

5 _____

🔊 Now listen again, and for questions 6–10, complete the sentences.

6 Speaker One says his dad is a fantastic _____ .

7 Speaker Two often _____ TV there.

8 Speaker Three does his _____ there.

9 Speaker Four has a _____ every morning.

10 Speaker Five says there are a lot of _____ on the walls.

Listening	10
Speaking	10
Test total	80

Please note that the audio material for the Listening test is on the Class Cassettes/CD.

Messages 1 PHOTOCOPIABLE © Cambridge University Press 2005 Module 4 test

6 Speaking

a Two students answer your questions.

● Greet Students A and B and ask them how they are.

● Ask each student questions about where they live, for example, *Where do you live? Do you live in a house or a flat? What can you see from your bedroom window?*. This is to introduce the topic of neighbourhood and towns.

b Two students talk to each other.

● Give both Student A and Student B a copy of the town map. Explain that they should take it in turns to ask one another for the location of various places (*shopping centre, park, museum* etc.) on the map (to practise prepositions: *in, behind, in front of, next to, opposite, on the right, on the left* etc.). There are twelve places highlighted.

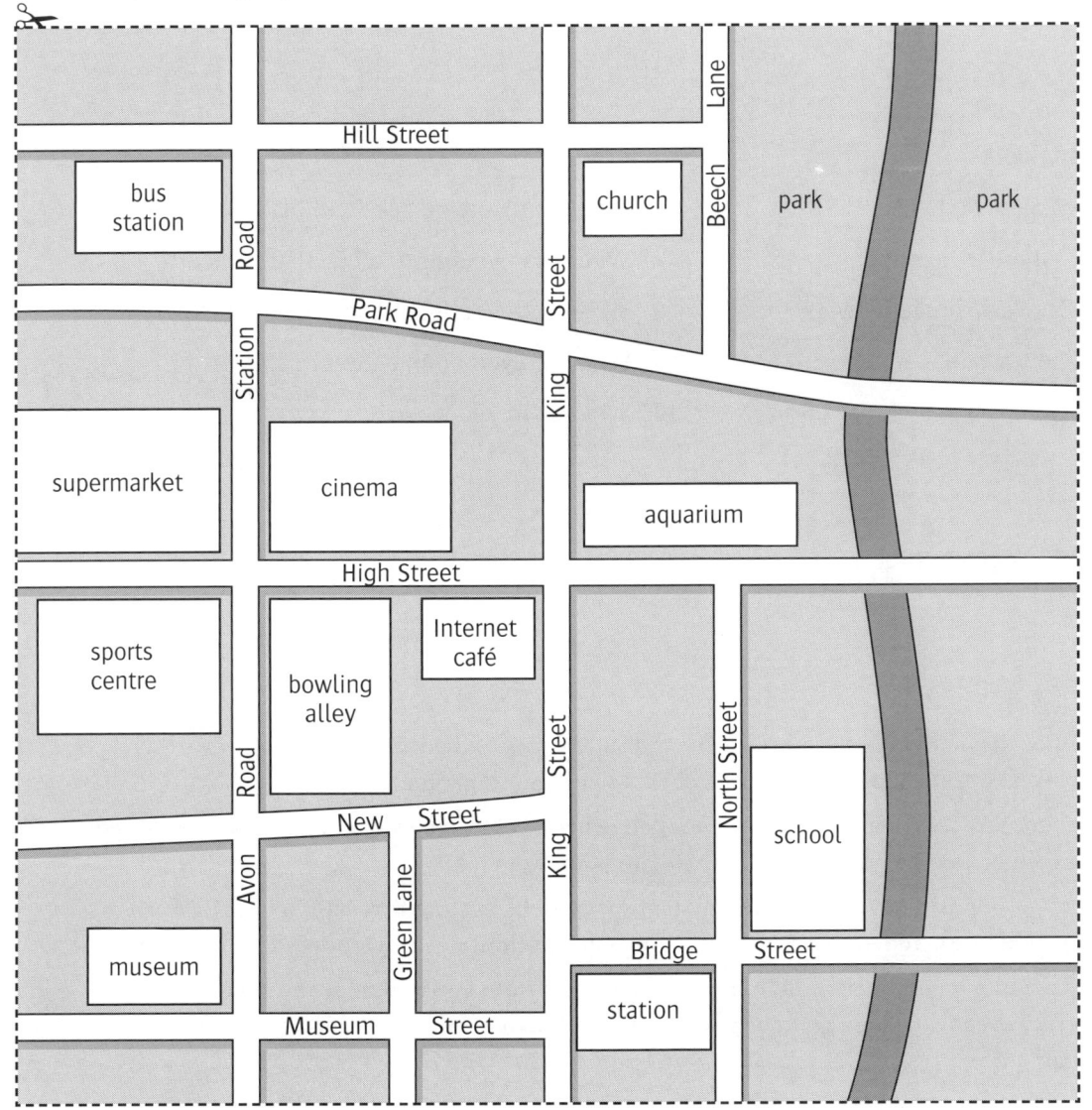

1 Grammar

a 1 c 2 a 3 b 4 c 5 c 6 a 7 b 8 a 9 b 10 a

b 1 There aren't 2 there isn't 3 There's 4 Are there 5 there isn't 6 Is there
7 There aren't 8 There are 9 there are 10 There isn't

2 Vocabulary

a 1 rug 2 wardrobe 3 mirror 4 clock 5 chest of drawers 6 shelf 7 lamp 8 radio
9 desk 10 chair

b 1 Internet café 2 bowling alley 3 sports centre 4 park 5 swimming pool
6 shopping centre 7 supermarket 8 cinema 9 tennis court 10 museum

3 Reading

Suggested answers:

1 Where does Sam/he live?

2 Where's / Where is Prague?

3 Where do Sam's/his parents work?

4 Why does he want to learn Czech?

5 How many rooms has their flat got?

6 What can Sam/he see from his bedroom window?

7 Where can you go to a classical concert?

8 Where can you learn about Czech history?

9 What can you do in a street café?

10 Where can you walk?

4 Writing

Check individual answers.

5 Listening

Tapescript

1 It's the heart of the house. We always eat there and sit and talk at the table. My dad's always there because he loves cooking and he's a fantastic cook. I help him sometimes.

2 I love this room because it's my room. I can go there when I want to be alone, when I want to listen to music or read. I often lie on my bed in the evenings and watch TV.

3 We've got a new television, DVD and video system so we all like sitting here after school or work. I also do my homework in here because there's a big table in front of the window so it's very light.

4 This is my favourite room! I have a shower every morning before I go to school and I have a nice long bath every evening before I go to bed. My brothers think I'm crazy but when I'm in the bath I can think and dream!

5 We only use this room when we have visitors for dinner or when we have a special meal for someone's birthday or when it's New Year. It's a cold room but I like it because there are a lot of photos of our family on the walls. Some of them are very old but they're all very interesting.

1 kitchen 2 bedroom 3 living room 4 bathroom 5 dining room 6 cook 7 watches
8 homework 9 shower 10 photos/photographs

6 Speaking

Check individual answers.

1 Grammar

a Complete the sentences. Circle the right answer: a, b or c.

0 Why are you looking at .... ?

 a I   b my   ©me

1 A: Are Chris and Robbie playing football?

 B: Yes, ...

 a they do   b they are   c they're

2 .... buy a new jacket this afternoon.

 a I'm going to   b I'm   c I'm going

3 What .... doing?

 a Paul is   b Paul's   c is Paul

4 Why don't you come with .... ?

 a us   b our   c we

5 What are you doing .... Saturday?

 a in   b at   c on

6 .... go to the cinema.

 a Shall we   b Let's   c Why don't we

7 A: Are you going to meet Alex this evening?

 B: No, ...

 a I aren't   b I'm not   c I don't

8 What .... the weather like in Spain now?

 a is   b does   c has

9 Where's my dictionary? I can't see ....

 a her   b him   c it

10 We're .... a test at the moment.

 a going to do   b doing   c do

[10]

b Present continuous or present simple? Put the verbs in the right form.

0 Jim _____likes_____ horror films. (*like*)

1 Jack _____ football this afternoon. (*play*)

2 Where _____ Jane _____ ? (*live*)

3 A: Where's Sarah?

 B: She _____ her homework upstairs. (*do*)

4 Tom often _____ to the cinema. (*go*)

5 I want to go out but it _____ . (*rain*)

6 What _____ you _____ next weekend? (*do*)

7 Look! Susie _____ her new dress. (*wear*)

8 Daniel _____ TV every evening. (*watch*)

9 I _____ a birthday party on Saturday. (*have*)

10 We always _____ the bus to school. (*get*)

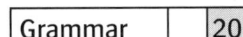

Grammar	20

[10]

2 Vocabulary

a Complete the sentences. Circle the right answer: a, b or c.

0 .... a minute!

  a Hang   b Hang in   ⓒ Hang on

1 This is a very good football ....

  a match   b play   c goal

2 Why are you .... that big bag?

  a wearing   b having   c carrying

3 We're going to an Italian restaurant ....

  a this evening   b this night   c this day

4 It's very .... today.

  a sunning   b sunny   c sun

5 What's your favourite football .... ?

  a score   b team   c support

6 We're going on holiday ....

  a tomorrow   b the next day   c the next week

7 It's very sunny. I can't see. Where are my .... ?

  a sandals   b shorts   c sunglasses

8 My hands are cold. I need my ....

  a gloves   b boots   c socks

9 Don't .... ! I can hear you.

  a say   b shout   c talk

10 I never .... trainers.

  a carry   b run   c wear

 10

b Label the pictures.

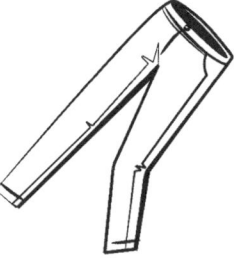

0 <u>trainers</u>   1 _____   2 _____   3 _____

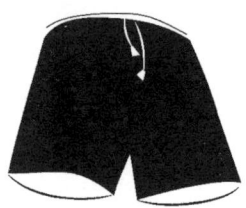

4 _____   5 _____   6 _____   7 _____

8 _____   9 _____   10 _____   10

Vocabulary 20

3 Reading

Read this page from Sally's diary.

31st December

I'm sitting in my room, listening to my favourite CD and thinking about next year. My parents are sitting downstairs with their friends. I can hear them – they're laughing and talking. They're having a party because tomorrow is the beginning of a new year.

I'm happy because it's the end of the year! I want next year to be different! I'm going to do my homework every day. I don't like school, but I want to have a good job so I know it's important to study. I'm not very good at maths or English now, but I'm going to be good at them! And I'm not going to watch television every evening, only at the weekend. I'm going to do sport with my friends. They play tennis and go bowling every week. I'm quite lazy so it's going to be difficult for me.

In the summer I'm going to visit my cousins in the USA. My parents are staying here so I'm going to travel alone. I know I'm going to have a fantastic time.

Every year I have lots of plans and good intentions but this year is going to be different! In one year I'm going to read my diary again ...

Are these sentences true, false or 'we don't know'? Circle the right answer: a, b or c.

0   It's nine o'clock in the evening.

    a true b false ©we don't know

1   Sally is in the living room.

    a true b false c we don't know

2   Her parents are in the dining room.

    a true b false c we don't know

3   They're happy.

    a true b false c we don't know

4   Next year Sally is going to do her homework at the weekend.

    a true b false c we don't know

5   She's going to get a good job.

    a true b false c we don't know

6   She doesn't like geography.

    a true b false c we don't know

7   It's going to be difficult to do lots of sport.

    a true b false c we don't know

8   Sally's going to the USA with her cousins.

    a true b false c we don't know

9   Her parents are going to the USA too.

    a true b false c we don't know

10   Sally writes in her diary every year.

    a true b false c we don't know

Reading	10

MODULE 5 TEST   **UNITS 9–10**

4 Writing

Read this email from Nick.

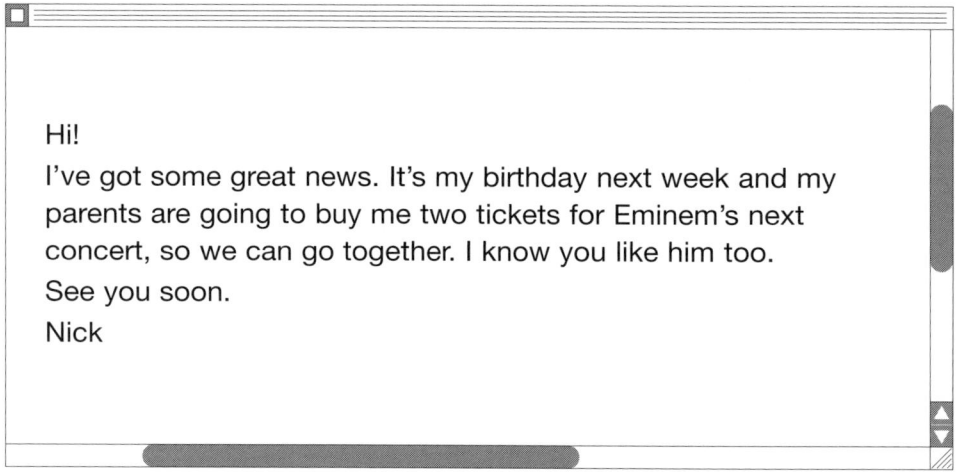

Hi!
I've got some great news. It's my birthday next week and my parents are going to buy me two tickets for Eminem's next concert, so we can go together. I know you like him too.
See you soon.
Nick

It's your birthday. Write an email to a friend and tell them what you are going to do. Write 25–35 words.

| Writing | 10 |

5 Listening

Name _____

Class _____ Date _____

Listen to Michael and Jane talking about their plans.
For questions 1–5, circle the right answer: a, b or c.

1 Michael is working in his _____ office.

   a mother's   b brother's   c father's

2 Jane _____ it.

   a can't believe   b can't understand   c can see

3 Michael's brother is a(n) _____ teacher.

   a German   b French   c English

4 Michael is going to Japan in a _____ .

   a week   b month   c year

5 Jane's parents are going to _____ .

   a give her driving lessons   b give her a car   c go on holiday

Now listen again and, for questions 6–10, complete the sentences.

6 Michael thinks his work is _____ .

7 Michael's going to work for another _____ .

8 Jane thinks that Tokyo is a really _____ .

9 Jane wants to go to on holiday to Spain in _____ .

10 Jane's _____ are going to be in Spain.

Listening	10
Speaking	10
Test total	80

Please note that the audio material for the Listening test is on the Class Cassettes/CD.

6 Speaking

a Two students answer your questions.

● Greet Students A and B and ask them how they are.

● Ask each student questions about future plans, for example, *What are you doing after school today? What are you going to do in the summer/winter holidays?*. (The students are to practise the future with the present continuous and *going to*.)

b Two students talk to each other.

● Give Student A a copy of card A and give Student B a copy of card B. Explain that they each have a page from a diary with their arrangements written down – it's the school holidays. They need to find a time to meet for a chat as they haven't seen each other for ages. They should take it in turns to suggest/reject a time (using the language of suggestion: *Let's …, Shall we ?, Why don't we …?*) until they can find a time that is mutually convenient. They should then arrange a time and a place.

A Talk to your partner. Find a time when you can meet for a coffee.

Sunday	11 am tennis with Anna	3 pm cinema with Mum
Monday		
Tuesday	10 am shopping with Aunt Sue	
Wednesday		2.30 pm swimming
Thursday	12 pm lunch with Liz and Emma	
Friday		4 pm music lesson
Saturday	visiting cousins – all weekend	

B Talk to your partner. Find a time when you can meet for a coffee.

Sunday		
Monday	10.30 am dentist	2 pm bowling with Alan
Tuesday		2.30 pm guitar lesson
Wednesday	helping Dad all day	
Thursday	My birthday - day out in London	
Friday		3 pm volleyball practice
Saturday	cousins staying all weekend	

1 Grammar

a 1 b 2 a 3 c 4 a 5 c 6 b 7 b 8 a 9 c 10 b

b 1 's/is playing 2 does, live 3 's/is doing 4 goes 5 's/is raining
6 are, doing 7 's/is wearing 8 watches 9 'm having 10 get

2 Vocabulary

a 1 a 2 c 3 a 4 b 5 b 6 a 7 c 8 a 9 b 10 c

b 1 hat 2 skirt 3 trousers 4 raincoat/coat 5 scarf 6 shorts 7 belt
8 socks 9 sandals 10 sweater

3 Reading

1 b 2 c 3 a 4 b 5 c 6 c 7 a 8 b 9 b 10 c

4 Writing

Check individual answers.

5 Listening

Tapescript

MICHAEL: Hi, Jane. How are you?

JANE: Fine, thanks. It's good to see you again. What are you doing these days?

MICHAEL: Well, at the moment I'm working in my dad's office. His secretary is on holiday so I'm helping him.

JANE: Really? I can't see you in an office!

MICHAEL: Why not? It's very interesting and I'm busy all the time.

JANE: How long are you going to be there?

MICHAEL: For another three weeks.

JANE: And what are you going to do then?

MICHAEL: I'm going to visit my brother. He's living in Tokyo at the moment.

JANE: What's he doing there?

MICHAEL: He's teaching English.

JANE: Wow! That's fantastic. I'd like to go to Japan and visit Tokyo – it's a really exciting city.

MICHAEL: Yes. I'm leaving in a month. But what about you?

JANE: Everything's fine. I'm having driving lessons at the moment because my parents say they're going to buy me a car when I can drive. I can't wait!

MICHAEL: What about the holidays?

JANE: I want to go to Spain in July because my aunt and uncle are going to be there, but I don't know.

MICHAEL: Well, have fun and good luck with the driving! See you soon.

JANE: Yeah, and have a good time in Japan. Bye.

MICHAEL: Bye.

1 c 2 a 3 c 4 b 5 b 6 interesting 7 three weeks
8 exciting city 9 July 10 aunt and uncle

6 Speaking

Check individual answers.

1 Grammar

Name ....

Class .... Date ....

a Complete the sentences. Circle the right answer: a, b or c.

0 Who .... Marilyn Monroe?

a were (b) was c did

1 A: Was Ben at Susan's party?

B: No, he ....

a weren't b wasn't c didn't

2 Did Jack .... his grandparents on Sunday?

a visited b visits c visit

3 I .... a stomache ache yesterday.

a had b had got c 'd

4 John was very hungry so he .... two pizzas for dinner!

a eats b ate c didn't eat

5 There .... any interesting books in the library.

a wasn't b were c weren't

6 What .... at school yesterday?

a did you do b you did c did you

7 A: Did Alice know the answer?

B: Yes, she ....

a knew b did c didn't

8 We had an English test .... afternoon.

a last b the last c yesterday

9 A: Were you late again this morning?

B: ....

a Yes, I was. b Yes, I were. c No, I weren't.

10 There .... a good programme on TV at ten o'clock.

a weren't b was c were

[10]

b Make affirmative sentences.

0 I didn't see you yesterday.   *I saw you yesterday.* ....

1 We didn't eat breakfast this morning.

2 Mark didn't come to my party.

3 I didn't see Julia at school yesterday.

4 Fiona didn't go to the cinema on Saturday.

5 Matthew didn't enjoy the concert.

6 My parents didn't leave at six o'clock.

7 Sarah didn't know the answer.

8 Duncan didn't speak French when he was six.

9 I didn't pack my bag yesterday.

10 Amy didn't have a headache last night.

[10]

| Grammar | 20 |

2 Vocabulary

a What are these occupations? Put the letters in the right order and make words.

0 torca   _____*actor*_____

1 straces   _____

2 lipto   _____

3 crathee   _____

4 trewir   _____

5 ifml rats   _____

6 rexpolre   _____

7 olosgozit   _____

8 antripe   _____

9 grenis   _____

10 tenistics   _____   [10]

b Complete the sentences with words from the box.

best friend   scientist   in a bad mood   president   What's the matter?
library   actor   last night   Sports Days   yesterday morning   last year

0 James was my ___*best friend*___ at primary school.

1 A: _____

   B: I've got a headache.

2 I had eggs for breakfast _____ .

3 John went to bed at eleven o'clock _____ .

4 I didn't enjoy _____ at school because I wasn't good at sport.

5 John F Kennedy was a famous _____ .

6 I'm _____ because we've got a lot of homework.

7 I really like our _____ . It has got lots of good books for teenagers.

8 Brad Pitt is my favourite Hollywood _____ .

9 I started my new school in September _____ .

10 I'm interested in chemistry and I want to be a _____ .   [10]

Vocabulary [20]

3 Reading

Read the text.

My grandparents came from a small town in England. They moved from England to Australia in 1959. They were married and they had one child, a boy called John (my father). They wanted to leave England because their life wasn't very good. They didn't have any money because my grandfather didn't have a job and my grandmother didn't work because their little boy was only five years old.

So they started a new life in Sydney. From the first day, they loved the city and they loved the sea and the beaches. Everything was so clean and the people were all so friendly. The weather was fantastic, warm and sunny every day, very different from the grey, wet days in England.

John started school and soon he had lots of new friends. In fact, his best friend, Josh, was also from England. Granddad and Grandma started new jobs and they had another child. This time it was a little girl, my Aunt Barbara.

When John was eighteen, he knew he wanted to go back to England to see it again. So he packed his bags and left his home and his family. He liked what he saw so he stayed there. He went to university and studied to become a teacher. Now he teaches at my school, but he doesn't teach me!

Now answer the questions.

0 Where did the writer's grandparents come from?

They came from a small town in England.

1 When did they move?

....

2 Where did they move to?

....

3 Were they married?

....

4 Why didn't they have any money?

....

5 How old was John when they moved?

....

6 What was the weather like in Australia?

....

7 What was their daughter called?

....

8 When did John go back to England?

....

9 Why did he go back to England?

....

10 What does John do now?

....

| Reading | 10 |

4 Writing

Read this email from Rachel.

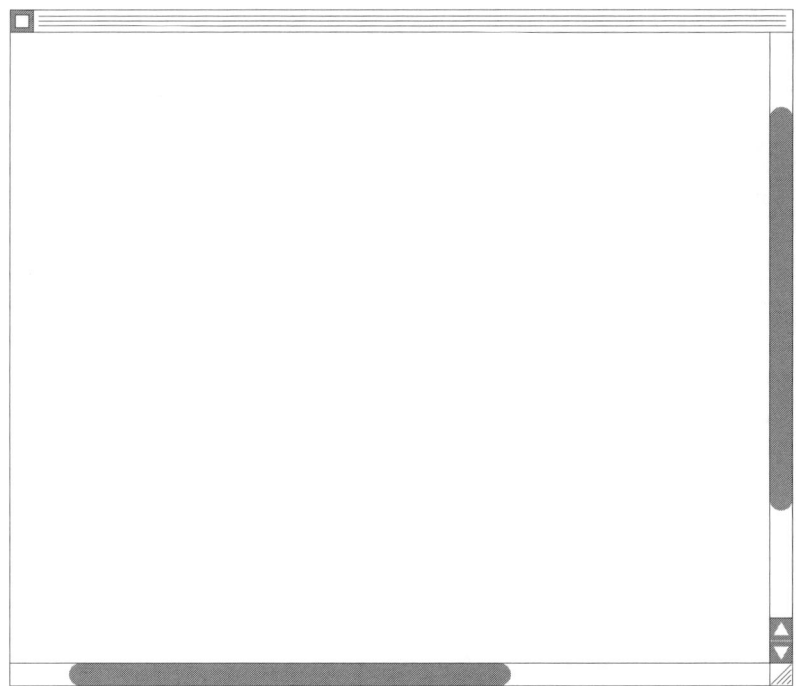

Hi!

I hope you're well. I know it was your birthday last week. Happy Birthday! Sorry I'm late but I wasn't near a computer on the day. What did you do?

What presents did you get? Did you have a party? Did you go out with your friends?

Please write soon and tell me everything!

Lots of love

Rachel

Write an email to Rachel. Answer her questions. Write 25–35 words.

Writing	10

5 Listening

🔊 Listen to Declan and Laura. For questions 1–5, are the sentences true (T) or false (F)? Tick (✔) the right answer.

1 Declan loves his job.   T........   F........

2 He's working at a secondary school.   T........   F........

3 He doesn't like children.   T........   F........

4 The children are ten years old.   T........   F........

5 Laura wants to be a pop star.   T........   F........

🔊 Now listen again and, for questions 6–10, complete the sentences.

6 Declan says the children are ....

7 Laura's going to meet a .... producer.

8 She knows he will .... her music.

9 Declan wants to go to all the ....

10 Laura suggests meeting for a ....

Listening	10
Speaking	10
Test total	80

Please note that the audio material for the Listening test is on the Class Cassettes/CD.

Messages 1 PHOTOCOPIABLE © Cambridge University Press 2005 Module 6 test

6 Speaking

a Two students answer your questions.

- Greet Students A and B and ask them how they are.

- Ask each student questions about the schools they have been to, for example,
  When did you start at this school? Where did you go to school before? Did you like your primary school?.

b Two students talk to each other.

- Give Student A a copy of card 1A and give Student B a copy of card 1B. Explain that Student B has a photo of their last holiday. Student A should ask questions about the holiday using the prompts on their card. Encourage the students to be as expansive as possible and focus on the correct use/form of the past tense.

- Give Student B a copy of card 2A and give Student A a copy of card 2B. They should now reverse the roles and Student B should ask Student A questions.

1A You want to know about your partner's last holiday. Ask questions, using *Wh-* question words:

Where ...?

When ...?

Who ...?

What ...?

Why ...?

1B

2A You want to know about your partner's last holiday. Ask questions, using *Wh-* question words:

Where ...?

When ...?

Who ...?

What ...?

Why ...?

2B

---

1 Grammar

a 1 b 2 c 3 a 4 b 5 c 6 a 7 b 8 c 9 a 10 b

b
1 We ate breakfast this morning.
2 Mark came to my party.
3 I saw Julia at school yesterday.
4 Fiona went to the cinema on Saturday.
5 Matthew enjoyed the concert.

6 My parents left at six o'clock.
7 Sarah knew the answer.
8 Duncan spoke French when he was six.
9 I packed my bag yesterday.
10 Amy had a headache last night.

2 Vocabulary

a 1 actress 2 pilot 3 teacher 4 writer 5 film star 6 explorer 7 zoologist 8 painter
9 singer 10 scientist

b 1 What's the matter? 2 yesterday morning 3 last night 4 Sports Days 5 president
6 in a bad mood 7 library 8 actor 9 last year 10 scientist

3 Reading

1 They moved in 1959.
2 They moved to Australia.
3 Yes, they were.
4 Because his grandfather didn't have a job (and his grandmother didn't work).
5 He was five (years old).

6 It was fantastic / warm and sunny every day.
7 She was called Barbara.
8 He went back to England when he was eighteen.
9 Because he wanted to see it again.
10 He's a teacher.

4 Writing

Check individual answers.

5 Listening

Tapescript

DECLAN: Hello, Laura! How are you?

LAURA: Hi, Declan! I'm fine. How about you?

DECLAN: Well, I'm really happy at the moment because I've got a new job.

LAURA: Yeah? What are you doing now, then?

DECLAN: I'm working as a teacher.

LAURA: Is it a primary school or a secondary school?

DECLAN: Primary. The children are fantastic.

LAURA: How old are they?

DECLAN: They're seven and eight. Anyway, what about you? Are you still trying to be a pop star?

LAURA: Yes! In fact, next week I'm going to meet a famous producer from a big record company.
I know he's going to love my music.

DECLAN: Well, have fun. I'd like to have a famous friend! We can go to all the parties and meet the stars.

LAURA: Why don't we have a coffee next week after my meeting and I can tell you all about it?

DECLAN: Great idea. See you then.

LAURA: Bye.

1 T 2 F 3 F 4 F 5 T 6 fantastic 7 famous 8 love 9 parties 10 coffee

6 Speaking

Check individual answers.

1 Grammar

Name ....
Class .... Date ....

a Complete the sentences. Circle the right answer:
a, b or c.

0 There .... any bread on the table.

   (a) isn't   b is   c aren't

1 A: What .... your friends like?

   B: They're great.

   a do   b are   c can

2 You .... talk in the library because people

   are studying.

   a must   b can   c mustn't

3 We .... often late for school.

   a are   b come   c go

4 Do you like .... trainers? I bought them yesterday.

   a that   b this   c these

5 A: Does Jake play tennis?

   B: No, ...

   a he don't   b he doesn't   c he doesn't play

6 Do you want to come to the cinema with .... ?

   a us   b our   c we

7 A: Have Dave's parents got a new car?

   B: Yes, ...

   a they've got   b they do   c they have

8 Sarah .... her friends after school yesterday.

   a is meeting   b met   c meets

9 There's .... spaghetti in the cupboard.

   a any   b some   c a

10 A: Where's Steve?

    B: He .... a shower.

    a has   b had   c is having

[10]

b Complete the sentences with the right form of the verbs in the box.

| study not speak know buy have not eat be meet drink do play |

0 I *'m going to study* English at university next year.

1 Alex .... some new trousers last weekend.

2 The children .... in the garden at the moment.

3 Where .... you last night?

4 John .... all the answers because he studies every day.

5 A: When .... you .... your husband?

   B: In 1999.

6 A: What .... you .... this weekend?

   B: Oh, not much.

7 Next year I .... a big party for my 18th birthday!

8 I was very thirsty so I .... a litre of water.

9 I .... meat because I'm a vegetarian.

10 .... Spanish to Kate! She doesn't understand it.

[10]

| Grammar | 10 |

FINAL TEST

2 Vocabulary

Name ....

Class .... Date ....

a Complete the sentences. Circle the right answer: a, b or c.

0   How are you?

   (a) All right, thanks.   b I'm twelve.   c I'm John.

1   My sister's very .... in cooking.

   a good   b bad   c interested

2   Germany is a ....

   a nationality   b country   c language

3   The day after Tuesday is ....

   a Monday   b Wednesday   c Friday

4   My aunt's husband is my ....

   a uncle   b cousin   c grandfather

5   My brother is always .... a bad mood in the mornings.

   a in   b on   c under

6   Susan's very .... She plays a lot of sports.

   a energetic   b lazy   c helpful

7   The weather's awful today. It's really ....

   a sunny   b foggy   c warm

8   My feet are so cold. Where are my new .... ?

   a gloves   b sandals   c socks

9   Philip's got .... hair.

   a tall   b small   c straight

10   What time did you go to bed .... ?

   a yesterday night   b last night   c tonight

| 10 |

b Match the verbs in A with nouns in B.

A		B
0	play	a	money
1	go	b	a photo
2	wait	c	the Net
3	wear	d	a horse
4	join	e	a minute
5	catch	f	swimming
6	ride	g	a bag
7	take	h	volleyball
8	spend	i	a bus
9	pack	j	a club
10	surf	k	glasses

0 *h*   1 ....   2 ....   3 ....   4 ....   5 ....   6 ....   7 ....   8 ....   9 ....   10 ....

| 10 |

| Vocabulary | 20 |

3 Reading

Read this text about Emma.

When I left university, I wanted to travel so I went to South Africa to visit friends and family. I loved it there because the country is very interesting and the people are very friendly, but after a year I came back to England and trained to be an English teacher. My first job was in Germany in a small school where my students were adults and children (but not in the same class!). At first, it was very difficult because there were a lot of things I didn't know. My classes were usually in the morning and in the evening so I had the afternoon to think about my lessons. I loved the job because everything was new and exciting and my students were very kind to me. Sometimes we went to a restaurant or café and they practised their English and I practised my German.

I lived in Germany for two years and then I left because I wanted to see other countries. I was very sad to go but I knew it was time to leave. My next job was in Bulgaria. It's a beautiful country next to Greece, Turkey and Romania. My life there was very different because I was the only English person in the town so everybody knew me! I was a teacher at a secondary school and in my first year there I had lessons with every student in the school. It was very difficult to remember everyone's name because I had hundreds of students! My life there was very busy so I didn't really have enough time to learn the language, but I did my best and I can still remember some words today.

I'm living in England again now and I'm not teaching, but I often think about those jobs and all the great students I had.

Are these sentences true, false or 'we don't know'? Circle the right answer.

0   Emma went to university in South Africa.

   a true   ⓑ false   c we don't know

1   She lived in South Africa for a year.

   a true   b false   c we don't know

2   She loved the weather in South Africa.

   a true   b false   c we don't know

3   She had a job as an English teacher when she came back to England.

   a true   b false   c we don't know

4   Her first job was boring.

   a true   b false   c we don't know

5   She sometimes spoke German with her students.

   a true   b false   c we don't know

6   She left Germany because she didn't like it.

   a true   b false   c we don't know

7   Her second job was with teenagers.

   a true   b false   c we don't know

8   She didn't remember everyone's name.

   a true   b false   c we don't know

9   She can speak a little Bulgarian.

   a true   b false   c we don't know

10 Emma's teaching in England now.

   a true   b false   c we don't know

Reading	10

FINAL TEST

4 Writing

You get this email from Jane.

Hi!
Guess what! I went to the cinema to see the new
Harry Potter film with my parents at the weekend.
It was fantastic! The time went so quickly because it
was so exciting. I really want to read the book now.
Write soon.
Love
Jane

You went to the cinema at the weekend too. Write an email to Jane
and tell her about the film you saw. Write 25–35 words.

| Writing | 10 |

Messages 1   PHOTOCOPIABLE   © Cambridge University Press 2005   Final test

FINAL TEST

5 Listening

Listen to five people talking about different places in a town. For questions 1–5, write down the name of the place they are describing (for example: supermarket, bus station etc.).

1 ....

2 ....

3 ....

4 ....

5 ....

Listen again and, for questions 6–10, complete the sentences.

6 Speaker One likes the tropical .... best.

7 Speaker Two has got a return ....

8 Speaker Three is sitting at a ....

9 Speaker Four likes watching films in ....

10 Speaker Five says you mustn't take .... here.

Listening	10
Speaking	10
Test total	80

FINAL TEST

Please note that the audio material for the Listening test is on the Class Cassettes/CD.

6 Speaking

a Two students answer your questions.

- Greet Students A and B and ask them how they are.

- Tell students that it is near the end of the school year now. Ask each student questions about the past school year (using the past simple tense), for example, *What sports did you do? What subjects did you study?* The students are going to be talking about the past school year so any questions connected with that will be fine.

b Two students talk to each other.

- Give Student A a copy of card A and Student B a copy of card B. Explain that it is the end of the school year. They are going to be asking each other about their past school year and their next holiday. They should use the prompts on their cards to ask questions. Encourage them to take it in turns so that it sounds like a natural conversation. They can of course expand as much as possible!

A **Talk with your partner about the school year and plans for the holidays. Ask questions about:**

- favourite subjects and why

- things your partner enjoyed / didn't enjoy

- favourite teacher and why

- plans for the holidays

B **Talk with your partner about the school year and plans for the holidays. Ask questions about:**

- favourite subjects and why

- things your partner enjoyed / didn't enjoy

- favourite teacher and why

- plans for the holidays

FINAL TEST

Messages 1 PHOTOCOPIABLE © Cambridge University Press 2005 Final test

1 Grammar

a 1 b 2 c 3 a 4 c 5 b 6 a 7 c 8 b 9 b 10 c

b 1 bought 2 are playing 3 were 4 knows 5 did, meet
   6 are, doing 7 'm going to have 8 drank 9 don't eat 10 Don't speak

2 Vocabulary

a 1 c 2 b 3 b 4 a 5 a 6 a 7 b 8 c 9 c 10 b

b 1 f 2 e 3 k 4 j 5 i 6 d 7 b 8 a 9 g 10 c

3 Reading

1 a 2 c 3 b 4 b 5 a 6 b 7 a 8 c 9 a 10 b

4 Writing

Check individual answers.

5 Listening

Tapescript

1 I love coming here when I'm alone. It's dark and quiet and you can watch the fish swimming all day. I like the tropical fish best because they're so small and colourful – red, blue, orange, yellow, green – all the colours you can imagine.

2 I'm going to visit my grandparents today so I'm here waiting for my train. I've got a return ticket because I'm coming back this evening. I love travelling by train because I like reading and listening to music and you can look out of the window for hours.

3 I'm sitting at a computer now checking my emails. I've got lots of pen friends and we write to each other every week. It's very exciting to open up your inbox and see how many emails you've got! It's quite cheap here. There are lots of computers and you can have a cup of coffee while you surf the Net.

4 I usually come here at weekends. I'm very lucky because there's always a film that I want to see. The tickets are cheaper for students so it doesn't matter too much if the film isn't that good. I like watching films in French because it's my favourite subject.

5 This is a very special place. Most people come here to sit quietly but there are also a lot of tourists. When you walk round you mustn't take photographs and you must be quiet. A lot of people get married here.

1 aquarium 2 station 3 Internet café 4 cinema 5 church/cathedral
6 fish 7 ticket 8 computer 9 French 10 photographs/photos

6 Speaking

Check individual answers.

Acknowledgements

The publishers are grateful to the following contributors:

Fran Banks: editorial work
pentacorbig: text design and layouts

The publishers are grateful to the following illustrators:

Mark Duffin, F&L Productions, Sophie Joyce, Graham Kennedy, Kate Sheppard (c/o Beehive Illustration), Mike Gibby (c/o The Organisation), Lisa Smith (c/o Sylvie Poggio)

The publishers are grateful to the following photographic sources:

AA World Travel Library for p. 87(t); Punchstock / Goodshoot for p. 87(b).
Picture research by Kevin Brown